SALES TURNAROUND

A Playbook for
Growth and Revenue Performance

Mark C. Ward

Grosvenor House
Publishing Limited

This book is published by
Grosvenor House Publishing Ltd
Link House
140 The Broadway, Tolworth, Surrey, KT6 7HT.
www.grosvenorhousepublishing.co.uk

A CIP record for this book
is available from the British Library

ISBN 978-1-83615-088-6

Contents

PROLOGUE

The year was 2018. I rubbed my eyes wearily as the cab pulled up to the glossy high-rise that housed the headquarters of my latest client, a leading identity verification platform provider with head offices in San Jose, the largest city in Silicon Valley, widely considered to be the heart of the area. I was excited to find myself in one of the global epicentres of innovation. I had been brought in to lead a turnaround of their sales organisation because I had done something similar for one of their competitors in the UK. The company was dominant in its competitive market, led by a workaholic CEO who spearheaded an impressive growth trajectory fuelled by rapid acquisitions and an unrelenting push into new industry sectors and geographies. However, while product-market fit was strong, something was obviously very wrong. I was told that the sales capabilities were not keeping pace with ambitions and growth had plateaued. That of course was only the tip of the iceberg.

Stepping into the sleek lobby, after ascending in a glass lift, I was struck by the youthful energy and vibe. Initial conversations confirmed that they had grown rapidly in a short period of time, nearly tripling headcount after two major acquisitions. I saw in those initial meetings with the leadership team that their growing pains had been acute and now, with siloed teams, unclear strategies, poor use of their own data, and inefficient processes, their current and future growth was under grave threat. What concerned me the most during those initial impressions was something I had seen and worked with before and had come to dread: their acquisitions had been done very haphazardly and were nowhere near complete.

As the elevator whisked me down to ground that day, I experienced a suffocated tension in my chest coupled with typical excitement at the challenge of a new engagement. The tension was a familiar companion that I would describe as trepidation at both the immense effort required for success in the field of turnarounds and change, and the nuances of this company with its fragmented shards. But I had been down this road many times before, and I knew that with careful analysis, and a methodical and targeted turnaround programme supported by consistently excellent and wholehearted leadership, superb project communications and management, even the most dysfunctional of sales engines could be turned around. With a whole lot of luck some even get whipped into high-performance shape, but they are not the majority.

Over the next 4 weeks, I conducted stakeholder interviews, examined data and documents, and solidified my perspective in workshop forums on the root causes behind the company's sales struggles. A number of key problem areas stood out. While the company sat in an enviable position in the identity verification space, its sales organisation lacked cohesion and unity behind any coherent growth strategy. This was the first problem. The second was that the acquisition integrations were not only incomplete but done so poorly that the newly formed regional companies were competing against each other in the market and for internal resources. Mere siloes would have been preferable to the factions I encountered. Internal territorial conflicts were inevitable and ugly. All the usual benefits of merger or acquisition were being squandered. Tensions between sales teams in different geographies were so bad that contempt was being openly expressed in public forums. The sales organisation also directed feelings of resentment and frustration toward product, marketing, and the services teams. Their relationships too were frayed, with closed-door finger pointing rather than open communication and collective accountability.

I wish it stopped there. It didn't. The lack of integration had also led to major conflict over which technologies would be kept and which retired. With this ambiguity almost nobody committed to adoption of the CRM and ancillary applications. They were haemorrhaging productivity. Simple everyday workflows were broken, and sales operations, and the expected reporting, added little value to decision-making with no data-driven insights that could lead to any form of improvement.

The talent problem too was immense. For such a rapidly scaling business, their talent practices around hiring, onboarding, training, and retaining salespeople were remarkably informal. That is too charitable. Lackadaisical is a better term. A combined induction and onboarding journey of an entire week (!) was further undermined (hardly possible) with a shocking lack of sales assets and general enablement. Every problem you might imagine found its way into the metrics. Retention, time to target, percentage of sellers reaching target were all as low as you might imagine and then some. I won't go into root causes here but having a player-coach sales model was not only an unrealistic balancing act but a complete disaster. Sales meetings, pipeline reviews, and forecasting activities were labelled as a "shit show" by the CEO. Coaching was virtually non-existent outside of haphazard conversations lacking structure, consistency, or tie-in to actual sales activities.

As if the dysfunction was not enough, all of this was taking place in the context of major planned compensation plan changes intended to drive cross selling and recurring revenue. The first iterations had sparked resentment and lively protests due to perceived reduced earnings potential (they perceived right) and unacceptable levels of ambiguity around important thresholds and boundaries. Can you imagine pouring this fuel onto the already combustible situation? To say it exacerbated existing tensions between teams that already lacked sufficient trust and unity as a single collective sales engine would be an understatement.

Taken together, these issues posed an existential threat to this company's survival let alone its ambitious growth trajectory. The technology sector moves fast, and demand for identity verification solutions was, at that time, exploding. Without urgent course correction, they risked losing their hard-earned leadership position.

The report and scope of work I ended up drafting contained 73 specific recommendations, carefully sequenced in a 3-horizon plan. However, 5 key initiatives in horizon one formed the crux to catalyse rapid performance improvement. They included launching a Sales Turnaround Office. This internal team would drive implementation and change management for the turnaround effort. They would bring best practice structure while understanding cultural nuances. We would build a strategic sales operating and opportunity management blueprint. A codified blueprint would be an enormous integration boost and establish the platforms, rules of engagement, metrics, and processes to align teams strategically and operationally. We would optimise tools and data governance. Leveraging external expertise to overhaul the tech stack, enforce adoption via governance, enhance reporting, and clean data sets would begin to leverage the data and increase efficiency and insights. We would introduce a high-performance talent engine. Candidate sourcing and hiring methods, an onboarding programme, a sales training curriculum, and a team-based selling model would ramp up productivity. Finally, we would implement management systems. Implementing core sales meetings, analytics cadences, and coaching methodology would increase rigour, provide insights to sales leaders, and build capabilities across the team.

The initiatives and 3 horizons would unfold over 15 months. I proposed that the Programme be governed by a steering committee of senior leaders meeting bi-weekly to monitor progress and remove roadblocks. The turnaround office which I would Chair would manage workstreams, drawing upon product, technology, and process excellence resources in a collaborative model. External partners, us included, would be leveraged for design and tactical support around implementation and change management, sales operations, and systems optimisation. However, the solutions would be tailored to the company's unique culture and built for sustainable ownership by internal teams.

We agreed on a pilot approach prior to global rollout. The San Jose sales team would be the test group for initial changes given its size, maturity, and importance to revenue. After 90 days of intensive capability building, the new initiatives would be operationalised, equipping leaders and frontline sellers with the tools, knowledge and support frameworks needed for success. Mirroring Silicon Valley's obsession with failing fast to achieve product-market fit, the pilot would allow rapid iteration based on user feedback until the solutions were demonstrably effective.

With a successful pilot completed, plans were drawn up and rollout commenced across the rest of the US and Europe, before expanding to new continents. The turnaround office would provide tools and guides while collaborating virtually with regional teams. Regional launch events would inspire and align groups to the vision. Post-launch surveys would measure adoption, productivity lift, and seller satisfaction. Global adoption would take 12 months, allowing time for behavioural change and capability building while sales continued. But the promises were clear – growth and competitive dominance.

No major change programme ever goes smoothly from start to finish. And this client's turnaround was no exception. We faced three significant obstacles that threatened to derail progress. First, halfway through the programme, a new Human Resources Director joined the steering committee (SteerCo) overseeing the turnaround. Though ambitious, she lacked the historical context underpinning, and could not possibly yet grasp the systemic issues behind her new employer's sales dysfunction. Yet, she immediately began questioning elements of the scope and approach, requesting modifications before taking time to immerse herself in the intricacies of the sales engine analysis. Her requests risked undermining the interdependencies we had built into the initiatives and the judgement behind other decisions taken. Her confrontational style, while enviable (she was a force of nature), sowed doubts among other leaders. Tempers flared as doubt set in and momentum stalled. We entered another crisis period. I managed to convince the CEO to intervene and secure her cooperation by whatever means necessary. To support that we initiated a one-and-a-half-day deep dive to educate her on the imperatives behind the methodology we were using and necessity of our chosen design and scope. The workshop allowed her to vent concerns but ultimately, she bought in on the direction. I learned through that to bring new governing members onboard more methodically to avoid future disruption and a repeat of this pain, and to build this in as a contingency with cost implication so that it is commercially fair.

When the Channel and Group Marketing heads quit within a week of each other, right before our big launch, it felt like a punch to the gut. It hurt, and it left us scrambling. The senior team was split on how to handle it, and we had some pretty heated discussions about whether to stick to the plan or change course. I worked my hindquarters off with the CEO and a bunch of other leaders to keep things on track, but I'm not going to lie, it was a struggle. I even had to dust off my rusty Executive Search skills to help find replacements, which was the last thing I wanted to do. We found some people to fill the roles, but it was far from ideal.

To make matters worse, our private equity investors were all over us about the turnaround. They were constantly poking their noses in, questioning every decision and second-guessing the CEO. It was like they had no faith in the executive team. I was worried that all their meddling would derail the whole programme and leave everyone confused and frustrated. Behind the scenes, we tried to be diplomatic but firm in our responses, reminding them that this was our show to run. The CEO even had to have a sit-down with the Chairman, who's known for being a real tough cookie, to get them to back off. It helped, but it was just another reminder that turnarounds are never smooth sailing. There's always some hidden drama bubbling up to the surface.

We got there in the end, but I won't sugarcoat it. It was brutal, left me bruised and utterly depleted, and forced me to take a controversially long holiday to renew my enthusiasm and get my mojo back. My project team suffered too, and despite my best efforts to shield them from the rampant dysfunction, the anxious and abrasive stakeholders, the intense pressure on the scope and the boundaries we had in place, and the incessant changes requiring adaptation, I failed many times, this despite my experience, and the forceful nature I'm often told I have. "Why?" you might ask. Why was I unable to control the programme and the people enough to keep it on track and to execute as planned? Because that is not the way transformation goes. Ever. Transformational change of organisational systems always has elements of unpredictability, volatility and even chaos. Things emerge unexpectedly, out of nowhere. To attempt to control for all unpredictable emergence and turbulence would be a fool's errand. Rigid control is antithetical to the project of transformation.

To my team's credit, and thanks to their problem-solving brilliance and stoic resilience, they remained unbroken and like steel emerging from the crucible, hardened for the next round of battle with its unforeseen turbulence and trench warfare.

Eighteen months later, several of our goals had been achieved. Double-digit sales growth, a sharp rise in average order value, and a greatly improved close ratio underpinned by streamlined productivity, and a vibrant sales culture were some of the most delicious rewards. The turnaround seemed to some outsiders to happen overnight; just how wrong they were they will never know. I knew just how many gruelling days and long and sleepless nights it took to build and execute that programme and the many difficulties behind the scenes, with us facing into problem after problem.

The client had eventually risen to the challenge. Much credit goes to the CEO who steadied the ship and inspired belief and resolve during the many storms we faced. The sales team displayed unbelievable grit to push through the uncomfortable ambiguity and tremendous pain that accompanies real change and lasting growth.

Seeing the energy at the last sales kick-off I attended, led proudly by sales leadership brimming with purpose, almost made the addition of the grey hair that had sprouted and the long period of atrocious sleep data worthwhile. The sales engine was now propelling the business to new heights through aligned effort in an operating blueprint that was not only fit for purpose, but exceptional. This was a growth engine firing on all cylinders, well integrated, motivated and enabled. And I, and my small team – the "renegade band of brothers and sisters" as I jokingly called them, had learned from our inevitable mistakes, and healed most of our own self-inflicted wounds. The project ended with our mojo intact and our sense of mission – to transform even more organisations into high performance sales engines – sharpened.

As I walked out of the gleaming headquarters for the final time, I again wrestled with conflicting feelings. I'm an onward and upward kind of guy, so part of me was glad to be moving on. In reality, we all already had, with other projects underway and some even mature. That said, I couldn't help but feel a profound sense of accomplishment. The journey had been arduous, but the destination made it all worthwhile. We had not only transformed a struggling sales organisation into a well-oiled machine, but we had also proven to ourselves and our colleagues that with unwavering determination, strategic ingenuity, and a united team, even the most daunting challenges could be overcome. The future, as always, lay ahead, bright and full of promise. I took some comfort from knowing that this experience had equipped us all with the skills, resilience, and hunger to take on even greater transformations. As I stepped into the crisp Silicon Valley air, I couldn't help but smile. We had done it, and damn, it felt good. The team had already scattered to the winds, off to their next adventures, but I knew we'd always have this shared triumph. We made memories. I don't remember what I did next that day, but I likely convinced myself that it was time for a stiff drink and the letting off of some steam before diving headfirst into the next challenge.

FOREWORD ON AI

In the rapidly evolving world of sales, where the quest for excellence and innovation knows no bounds, it is no exaggeration to say that a new era has dawned on the back of a disruption that can best be described as profound—one that seamlessly integrates the power of artificial intelligence (AI) into the very fabric of the sales discipline and revenue functions. At the time of this writing, there is a surge in AI agents making decisions autonomously in go-to-market operations, and a dramatic increase in spending on AI agents. I have nonetheless taken a deliberate decision to omit a dedicated chapter on AI and sales in "Sales Turnaround". Not only is that a stand-alone book beyond the scope of this endeavour, but whilst AI has undoubtedly become an indispensable tool in modern sales practices, it is ultimately just that – a tool. The core tenets of effective sales turnarounds, such as leadership, strategy, process optimisation, and talent development, transcend any specific technology or trend. I would not wish to give the impression that I am downplaying just how awesome AI is so let me tell you why it has me so excited.

The Transformative Power of AI in Sales

In today's data-rich landscape, where information holds the key to unlocking unparalleled insights and opportunities, AI has become an indispensable ally for sales professionals. This is especially true of those striving to adopt Impact-Centric Selling®, the methodology I built and that is taught by Revenue Arc. The sheer volume and complexity of data available can be overwhelming, but AI possesses this otherworldly ability to assimilate, analyse, and derive meaningful patterns from vast information landscapes.

The advent of AI technology has ushered in two distinct but complementary capabilities: generative AI, which responds to specific prompts and enhances human tasks, and autonomous AI agents, which can independently monitor, analyse, and act on behalf of sales teams. These cutting-edge tools serve as potent accessories, empowering sales professionals to navigate the complexities of information with unrivalled ease and precision.

Embracing AI as a Necessity

In the modern sales landscape, AI is no longer an optional enhancement but a fundamental necessity. As the standards for sales excellence continue to rise, the adoption of AI has become a do-or-die proposition. Organisations that fail to embrace and integrate these transformative technologies risk being rendered impotent in an era where AI-powered productivity, insights, and efficiencies are the norm.

One of the most significant advantages is the automation of routine tasks and the optimisation of workflows. AI algorithms can effortlessly handle data entry, lead prioritisation, and administrative responsibilities, freeing up valuable time for sales professionals to focus on high-value activities such as building relationships and closing deals. This increased efficiency translates into heightened productivity and accelerated sales cycles.

Personalisation and Predictive Intelligence

Moreover, AI enables sales teams to deliver hyper-personalised customer experiences. By analysing vast amounts of customer data, including preferences, behaviour patterns, and transaction histories, AI algorithms can generate highly targeted and relevant recommendations. This level of personalisation fosters deeper connections with customers, enhancing trust and loyalty.

The emergence of autonomous AI agents is revolutionising how we approach buyer engagement. These agents can proactively monitor buyer behaviour, predict needs, and even handle routine interactions independently, ensuring that every touchpoint in the buyer's journey is meaningful and properly supported. This shift enables a more buyer-centric approach, where customers receive immediate, relevant assistance without waiting for human intervention.

Data-Driven Decision-Making and Collaboration

The integration of AI also facilitates data-driven decision-making. In the past, sales decisions often relied heavily on intuition and subjective judgement. However, with AI-powered analytics, sales teams can access real-time, objective data that informs their choices. From identifying the most promising leads to determining optimal pricing strategies, AI provides evidence-based recommendations that minimise guesswork and maximise results.

AI also enhances collaboration and knowledge-sharing within sales organisations. By creating centralised repositories of customer data, sales insights, and best practices, AI platforms enable seamless information exchange across teams and departments. This collaborative environment fosters a culture of continuous learning and improvement, where sales professionals can learn from each other's successes and failures, ultimately elevating the collective performance of the organisation.

Challenges and Considerations

It is important to recognise that the integration of AI into sales is not a replacement for human expertise and intuition. Rather, it is a powerful augmentation that amplifies the capabilities of sales professionals. The synergy between human intelligence and artificial intelligence creates a formidable force, where the creativity, empathy, and relationship-building skills of salespeople are complemented by the data-driven insights and efficiency of AI.

As we move towards a 'Human-in-the-Loop' sales model, where AI agents handle routine tasks and interactions, sales professionals are elevated to become orchestrators of the customer experience. They focus on complex negotiations, strategic relationship building, and situations requiring nuanced human judgement—areas where human expertise remains irreplaceable.

However, the adoption of AI in sales is not without its challenges. One of the primary concerns is the need for data privacy and security. As AI systems process vast amounts of sensitive customer information, organisations must prioritise robust data protection measures to maintain trust and comply with regulatory requirements. Additionally, the implementation of AI requires a significant investment in technology infrastructure and other resources to effectively leverage AI tools and interpret their outputs.

The bottom line then is that the integration of artificial intelligence into the age-old art of sales represents a pivotal moment in the evolution of the sales landscape. It is not merely a strategic advantage; it is an imperative for success in the modern business world. As AI continues to advance and permeate every aspect of sales, organisations that fail to adapt risk being left behind, whilst those that embrace and leverage its potential will soar to new heights of excellence and impact.

The future of sales belongs to those who harness the power of AI as a transformative tool, redefining the boundaries of what is possible and setting new standards for excellence. By seamlessly integrating AI into the very core of their sales processes, organisations empower their sales professionals to navigate the complexities of the digital age with unparalleled efficiency, intelligence, and impact. It is a paradigm shift that reshapes the sales landscape, delivering unrivalled value to customers and propelling businesses towards a brighter, more innovative future.

The Decision to Omit a Dedicated AI Chapter

My decision to omit a dedicated chapter on AI and sales in "Sales Turnaround" remains well-founded and reflects a deep understanding of the fundamental principles and strategies that drive successful sales transformations. Whilst AI has undoubtedly become an indispensable tool in modern sales practices, the core tenets of effective sales turnarounds transcend any specific technology or trend, no matter how disruptive. Until such a time as machines do the buying this will hold true.

By focusing on these foundational elements, the book provides readers with a timeless and universally applicable framework for revitalising sales performance. The principles and insights shared are not tied to any particular technological paradigm but rather emphasise the human factors and organisational dynamics that are essential for driving sustainable sales growth.

Moreover, the rapid pace of technological change means that any discussion of AI in sales risks becoming quickly outdated. By not dedicating a chapter to AI, I have decided to sidestep the pitfall of providing insights or recommendations that may lose their relevance as AI technologies continue to evolve. Instead, I've focused on the enduring strategies and best practices that sales leaders can adapt and apply in any technological context.

It is also important to recognise that the successful implementation of AI in sales requires a strong foundation of effective sales processes, data management, and organisational alignment. Without these fundamental building blocks in place, organisations may struggle to realise the full potential of AI-driven sales initiatives. By prioritising these core areas in the book, I provide readers with the necessary groundwork to leverage AI and other emerging technologies effectively.

Furthermore, in the context of turnaround, any integration of AI into sales processes is not a standalone solution but rather a component of a broader initiative. The principles and frameworks I present in this book, such as leadership alignment, go-to-market strategy, and performance management, create the necessary context and structure for AI to deliver meaningful results. By equipping readers with a comprehensive understanding of sales turnaround best practices, the book empowers them to incorporate AI and other technologies into their sales strategies in a way that drives genuine, long-term performance improvements.

INTRODUCTION

The complex interplay of human systems and organisational dynamics forms the bedrock of successful sales operations in the B2B landscape. This intricate dance of psychology, communication, and systems science underpins the revolutionary approach to sales transformation outlined in this book.

In the ever-evolving world of technology and B2B sales, the need for adaptable, efficient, and high-performing sales engines has never been more critical. Companies, regardless of their financial health or market position, cannot afford to overlook the vital importance of their sales function. It is the lifeblood of revenue generation, deal origination, and sustainable growth.

This concise volume distils decades of experience in transforming B2B sales engines into a comprehensive guide for enhanced performance and accelerated, sustainable growth. It focuses on seven critical, interconnected dimensions that demand thorough diagnostics and optimisation in any sales turnaround scenario: strategy, structure, processes, technology, culture, leadership, and talent development. The book recognises that these elements are inextricably linked, with changes in one invariably impacting the others.

Drawing from extensive experience in managing teams, selling, designing, and delivering complex sales turnaround programmes worldwide, this book offers invaluable insights gleaned from assessing sales organisations for private equity due diligence, conducting diagnostic exercises, and crafting detailed sales operation blueprints. It eschews unnecessary jargon and outdated data in favour of genuine, actionable insights that can drive real change in sales organisations.

Structured in four parts—Envision, Diagnose, Design, Implement—this book cuts through the noise and gimmicks often associated with sales literature.

This is more than just a book; it's a distillation of a career dedicated to sales excellence. It serves as a comprehensive guide through the intricate landscape of B2B sales transformation, offering readers the tools, strategies, and insights needed to revolutionise their sales engines.

Whether you are a sales leader looking to turbocharge your team's performance, a CEO seeking to transform your company's revenue generation, or a consultant aiming to deliver impactful change, this book provides the roadmap to navigate the complex terrain of modern B2B sales. It promises to challenge conventional thinking, inspire innovative approaches, and ultimately, drive unprecedented growth and success in the competitive world of B2B sales.

Prepare to embark on a journey that will reshape your understanding of sales transformation and equip you with the knowledge to lead your organisation to new heights of sales excellence.

PART ONE | ENVISION

Chapter 1: The System Imperative

The book begins by exploring systems thinking, an essential and unparalleled framework in modern business strategy. Systems thinking is crucial for comprehensive problem analysis and informs the design and scope of change programmes. It emphasises understanding the interconnected relationships within a business, allowing leaders to make informed decisions that align with the organisation's strengths and values while anticipating potential unintended consequences.

Systems thinking highlights that organisational performance is influenced by multiple, interconnected factors rather than isolated elements. For example, compensation, while important, interacts with other factors such as meaningful work, professional growth opportunities, recognition, a positive work culture, and a sense of belonging and purpose. These elements collectively create a more compelling employee value proposition than compensation alone.

Leadership and management practices also play a significant role in shaping employee satisfaction, performance, and retention. A positive organisational culture is essential, as even competitive compensation cannot offset the negative impact of poor leadership or an unsupportive environment. Retention and performance challenges require a holistic approach that considers all relevant factors, not just financial incentives.

Merely enhancing compensation is not sufficient to address broader organisational issues related to performance and retention. A systemic perspective is required to accurately diagnose and resolve these challenges, focusing on the overall employee experience and the interplay between various organisational factors. Adopting systems thinking allows organisations to implement more effective and sustainable solutions, avoiding the pitfalls of addressing symptoms rather than root causes.

Insights on Systems

Sales revenue engines are complex subsystems within broader organisational systems. They are cross-functional, encompassing interconnected roles, processes, and technologies that support sales opportunities. As open systems, they are dynamic and unpredictable, influenced by both internal and external factors.

These revenue engines, due to the unpredictable human behaviours and relationships within, manifest emergent properties that cannot be reliably anticipated. Instead of attempting to control such intricate systems, our focus should be on empowering them. Imposing our will on a system without understanding its inherent dynamics often leads to suboptimal outcomes. True optimisation involves listening to the system's feedback, discerning its patterns, and then fostering conditions for enhanced performance. Like mastering any complex skill, optimising a system requires risk-taking, vigilance, engagement, and adaptability. Effective navigation of these systems requires more than mere analytical skills; it calls for a holistic application of intellect, intuition, and other faculties.

A significant risk in optimising complex systems is making adjustments to one component that inadvertently impede the broader system. Sales leaders and consultants fall into this trap by focusing too narrowly on isolated metrics. For instance, changes to compensation structures can negatively affect collaboration and culture, or sales reorganisations might temporarily reduce revenues. The key is to approach interventions with a broad perspective, considering their ripple effects on culture, innovation, stability, and other vital aspects. Well-meaning quick fixes can lead to unintended negative consequences. Short-term changes for the collective good may sometimes clash with narrow interests. Leaders must manage these trade-offs holistically, remembering that the viability of the system as a whole depends on the interconnectedness of its components.

Summary Principles

- Organisations consist of interconnected components (subsystems) that work together towards a common goal. These subsystems, including marketing and sales, embody the principle of interdependence, encompassing all roles, systems, and processes supporting sales opportunities.

- Sales engines are complex, evolving, nonlinear systems characterised by inherent unpredictability. They demonstrate dynamic behaviour, often influenced by feedback loops that can amplify or dampen changes within the system, leading to nonlinear outcomes.

- The emergence of properties and the challenge of prediction are cornerstones of systems thinking. Emergent properties arise from the interactions of system components, leading to outcomes that cannot be predicted by examining the components alone. This unpredictability necessitates a shift from trying to control systems to understanding and influencing them.

- Optimising individual system components without considering the whole is suboptimal. This principle acknowledges that improvements in one part of the system can lead to adverse effects elsewhere, underscoring the importance of holistic thinking and the interdependencies within the system.

- Interventions lead to consequences, often unintended. Being blindsided by consequences is often a result of failing to appreciate the system's complexity and the interconnectedness of its parts. A comprehensive analysis and understanding of the system to mitigate such outcomes is essential.

- Management of the whole system and consideration of the long-term impacts of interventions reflect the systems thinking principle of synthesis over analysis.

Systems Actions | Tools | Best Practices

The systems thinking toolkit is vast. These six tools are invaluable:

1. **Stakeholder Mapping:** Create a comprehensive stakeholder map to identify all the key players, their roles, and their interconnections within the sales revenue engine. This visual representation will help leaders understand the complex web

of relationships and dependencies, ensuring a holistic approach to transformation.

2. **Process Mapping:** Develop detailed process maps of the sales engine, including all the steps, decision points, and handoffs between different functions. This will provide a clear understanding of how the system currently operates, identifying bottlenecks, inefficiencies, and areas for improvement.

3. **Feedback Loop Analysis:** Identify and analyse the key feedback loops within the sales engine, both positive and negative. A feedback loop is where one thing influences or causes a change in another which in turn changes something else. For example, a positive feedback loop in the sales engine could be increased sales success leads to higher motivation and engagement, which in turn drives even greater sales performance. Conversely, a negative feedback loop could be declining sales lead to lower morale and increased turnover, which further hampers sales performance. Understanding how these loops amplify or dampen changes will help leaders anticipate the potential unintended consequences of their interventions and make more informed decisions.

4. **Scenario Planning:** Engage in scenario planning exercises to explore the potential outcomes of different interventions on the sales engine. By considering multiple scenarios and their ripple effects on various aspects of the system, leaders can better assess the risks and benefits of each option and choose the most effective course of action.

5. **Cross-Functional Collaboration:** Foster cross-functional collaboration and communication throughout the transformation process. Establish regular meetings, workshops, or forums where representatives from different functions can share insights, discuss challenges, and align their efforts towards the common goal of optimising the sales engine.

6. **Continuous Monitoring and Adaptation:** Implement a system for continuous monitoring and adaptation of the transformation programme. Regularly collect and analyse data on key performance indicators, gather feedback from stakeholders, and assess the impact of interventions. Be prepared to make adjustments as needed to ensure the programme remains aligned with the overall goals and adapts to emerging challenges or opportunities.

PART ONE | ENVISION

Chapter 2: The Customer Journey Imperative

Building on the systems thinking principles discussed in Chapter 1, the customer journey represents a critical subsystem within the sales engine. Just as we examined how different components interact and influence each other in the broader sales system, understanding the customer journey requires analysing the intricate web of touchpoints, interactions, and feedback loops that shape customer experience and ultimately drive sales performance. While many organisations fixate on internal metrics and processes, my years in the field have shown that understanding and optimising the customer journey stands as perhaps the most critical foundation for sustainable transformation. The pain points that customers encounter - both visible and hidden - ripple through every sales metric, from initial engagement to renewal decisions, often in ways that remain frustratingly opaque to even the most experienced sales leaders.

I learned this lesson the hard way during a transformation project for a global software provider. The sales team was hitting their numbers, but customer churn was climbing steadily. As we dug deeper, we discovered that while the sales process appeared smooth, customers were struggling with a fragmented implementation process spanning multiple departments. The pain points in their post-purchase journey were creating a wave of dissatisfaction that eventually crashed back onto the sales team in the form of lost renewals and damaged reputation. This experience crystallised for me the vital importance of mapping and understanding the complete customer journey in any sales transformation initiative.

The B2B customer journey is far more complex than the linear progression that many envision. Instead, it represents an intricate web of interactions, touchpoints, and experiences that often span years. From the first spark of interest through to long-term partnership and advocacy, each stage presents unique challenges that directly influence sales performance. What makes this particularly challenging is that different departments often own different parts of the journey, creating potential gaps and disconnects that customers must navigate.

Understanding Pain Points Across the Journey

When examining customer journeys, we must look beyond surface-level frustrations to understand the deeper impact of pain points on both the customer and the organisation. Through countless transformation projects, I've developed a framework that evaluates pain points across three critical dimensions: Revenue Impact, Customer Experience Impact, and Operational Efficiency Impact. Each dimension is rated on a scale of 1-5, with 5 representing the most severe impact.

This framework has proved useful in helping my team and the organisations we serve prioritise their transformation efforts. For instance, a seemingly minor issue in contract processing might rate low on immediate revenue impact but score highly on customer experience and operational efficiency. When we understand these relationships, we can make more informed decisions about where to focus our transformation efforts.

The Journey Stages

The B2B customer journey encompasses many touchpoints that are best grouped into distinct stages, each presenting its own set of challenges and opportunities. The Discovery stage, where prospects first identify needs and begin exploring solutions, often suffers from information overload and poor alignment between marketing and sales messaging. During Evaluation, prospects frequently struggle with complex pricing structures and difficulty in comparing solutions effectively.

The Purchase stage, while seemingly straightforward, often hides significant friction in contract negotiations and approval processes. Legal vetting is often a painful bottleneck. Onboarding and Implementation stages frequently reveal disconnects between sales promises and delivery reality. Value Realisation - perhaps the most critical stage for long-term success - often lacks clear metrics and accountability.

Support and Renewal stages, which should be opportunities for strengthening relationships, too often become administrative burdens that erode customer satisfaction. The Advocacy Stage represents perhaps the most valuable yet often overlooked phase of the customer journey. In B2B environments, where complex solutions and long-term partnerships are the norm, customer advocates become powerful assets for organic growth. They not only provide references and referrals but also offer insights that can shape product development and go-to-market strategies. This stage deserves particular attention in any journey optimisation effort as it directly impacts both customer acquisition costs and lifetime value.

Each of these stages influences specific sales metrics, creating a complex web of cause and effect that must be understood for effective transformation. The interconnected nature of these stages exemplifies the systems thinking principles discussed in Chapter 1, where changes in one area inevitably ripple through to affect others.

Internal Echoes of External Pain

One of the most fascinating aspects of customer journey analysis is how internal pain points create or amplify external ones through a cascade effect. I witnessed this dramatically in a recent project where a poorly integrated CRM and contract management system was causing delays in quote generation. This internal inefficiency created frustrated prospects, extended sales cycles, and ultimately led to lost deals to more agile competitors.

What made this situation particularly interesting was how the impact rippled through the organisation. Sales teams, attempting to work around the system limitations, created manual processes that introduced errors and further delays. Customer success teams, handed incomplete or inaccurate information, struggled to deliver on implementation promises. The end result was a compound effect that turned what seemed like a simple systems integration issue into a significant drag on sales performance.

Cross-Functional Journey Optimisation Framework

The complexity of customer journey transformation mirrors the systemic nature of sales organisations discussed in Chapter 1.

Just as we cannot isolate individual components of the sales engine without considering their interconnections, we cannot rush the process of understanding and optimising the customer journey. This framework, which typically unfolds over several months, will later form a crucial input into the governance structures detailed in Chapter 10 and the pilot testing protocols outlined in Chapter 12.

The framework follows a strict hierarchy that many organisations, in their eagerness for quick fixes, often ignore: process optimisation must precede technology implementation, which in turn must precede capability development. This order aligns with the transformation sequence detailed in Chapter 11, where we explore comprehensive turnaround planning. I learned this lesson painfully during a turnaround for a global software provider, where an expensive CRM implementation failed to improve customer experience simply because the underlying processes were fundamentally broken. As one executive memorably put it, "We digitalised our problems rather than solving them."

Phase 1: Internal Journey Analysis

The first phase begins with what I call "deep listening" - creating space for every function to share their perspective on the customer journey. Through structured workshops, teams from sales, marketing, customer success, implementation, and support map their understanding of customer touchpoints and pain points. This approach directly feeds into the stakeholder engagement protocols we'll examine in Chapter 10, ensuring broad-based buy-in from the outset.

The workshops must capture not just the formal processes but also the informal workarounds that have evolved - these workarounds often reveal the most critical system breakdowns. The reconciliation of different departmental perspectives frequently uncovers surprising disconnects. In one recent project, we discovered that the sales team's "standard implementation timeline" promised to customers differed from the actual implementation team's timeline by nearly 60%.

Phase 2: Customer Experience Validation

Internal perspectives, no matter how comprehensive, must be validated against actual customer experience. I've learned through hard experience that organisations often develop blind spots about their own processes, convincing themselves that customers understand and accept various friction points that actually drive them to distraction.

This validation occurs through two parallel tracks:

Historical Analysis Track:

We conduct a systematic review of existing customer feedback sources, including:

- Customer support tickets and escalation records
- NPS survey responses and verbatim comments
- Customer success team meeting notes
- Sales opportunity post-mortems
- Social media mentions and online reviews
- Exit interviews from churned accounts

This historical analysis often reveals patterns that the organisation has either missed or grown accustomed to ignoring. In one transformation project, reviewing two years of support tickets uncovered that 40% of all escalations stemmed from a single process bottleneck that every department had simply accepted as "the way things work."

Direct Validation Track:

We conduct structured interviews with carefully selected customer segments:

- Recent customers who have completed implementation
- Long-term customers who have experienced multiple renewal cycles
- Customers who have recently churned
- Prospects who evaluated but didn't purchase
- Strategic accounts that represent ideal customer profiles
- High-growth accounts that have successfully scaled usage

The interview structure follows the customer journey but allows for organic exploration of pain points and workarounds that customers have developed. This often reveals surprising adaptations - in one case, we discovered that customers had created their own shadow tracking system because they didn't trust our implementation timeline updates.

Phase 3: Pain Point Analysis and Process Design

With both internal and external perspectives thoroughly documented, teams apply our three-dimensional impact framework introduced earlier in this chapter. This analysis directly informs the programme design principles we'll explore in Chapter 11, ensuring that process improvements align with broader transformation objectives.

During this phase, we often encounter the organisational inertia discussed in Chapter 3. People become invested in existing processes, however inefficient, and resistance to change can be strong. This resistance must be carefully managed through the governance structures and change management approaches detailed in Chapter 10.

The process design work completed here forms the foundation for the pilot programme design covered in Chapter 12. By thoroughly understanding current processes and their impact on customers before attempting changes, we create a solid baseline against which to measure pilot outcomes.

Phase 4: Technology Assessment and Integration Planning

Only after process improvements are clearly defined and validated do we turn to technology needs. This phase examines how existing systems can be better utilised or reconfigured to support new processes. The technology decisions made here must align with the broader transformation technology workstream detailed in Chapter 11.

This assessment feeds directly into the pilot testing protocols outlined in Chapter 12, where we'll need to carefully sequence technology changes to minimise disruption while maximising adoption. The integration planning completed during this phase also informs the rollout strategies we'll explore in Chapter 13.

Phase 5: Capability Development and Training Design

With validated processes designed and technology requirements identified, we can properly assess capability gaps. This phase involves creating detailed training plans, developing standard operating procedures, and establishing coaching frameworks. These elements feed directly into the capability building workstream discussed in Chapter 8 and the training protocols outlined in Chapter 12.

The capability framework developed here becomes particularly crucial during the programme rollout phase detailed in Chapter 13, where we'll need to scale training and support across the entire organisation. This framework must align with the broader performance management systems discussed in Chapter 10.

Phase 6: Implementation Planning and Governance Design

The final phase synthesises all previous work into a comprehensive implementation plan that includes:

- Initiative roadmaps with clear dependencies and milestones
- Metrics and measurement frameworks aligned with overall transformation KPIs
- Governance structures integrated with the broader transformation effort (Chapter 10)
- Stakeholder communication plans that feed into the broader change management strategy
- Resource allocation and budget requirements that inform the overall transformation budget

This plan becomes a crucial input into the steering committee governance detailed in Chapter 10 and directly shapes the pilot testing strategy outlined in Chapter 12. The governance structures established here must seamlessly integrate with the broader transformation governance framework while maintaining specific focus on customer journey optimisation.

The timeline appears extensive, but experience has shown that attempting to shortcut these phases invariably leads to superficial changes that fail to deliver sustainable improvement. Each phase builds upon the insights and validations of previous phases, ensuring that the final implementation plan addresses real rather than perceived problems, and delivers genuine value to customers rather than just internal efficiency.

Success Factors and Integration

The success of this framework depends heavily on its integration with the broader transformation protocols detailed in later chapters. Specifically:

- The governance structures established must align with the steering committee protocols in Chapter 10
- The metrics framework must feed into the broader performance management system
- The capability building approach must integrate with the training protocols in Chapter 12
- The implementation plan must align with the rollout strategies in Chapter 13

This systematic approach ensures that customer journey optimisation becomes a fundamental driver of the overall transformation, rather than a separate initiative. As we'll see in Chapter 10, success requires maintaining momentum through strong governance mechanisms while ensuring each phase builds logically on previous insights. The steering committee structure detailed later will play a crucial role in maintaining this momentum and ensuring proper resource allocation throughout the process.

By following this systematic approach and properly integrating it with the transformation protocols detailed in subsequent chapters, organisations can break free from the cycle of tactical fixes and achieve lasting improvements in customer experience. This lays crucial groundwork for the broader transformation journey we'll explore throughout the rest of this book.

The Power of Systematic Analysis

Breaking down these complex interconnections requires a systematic approach to journey analysis. In my experience, the most effective method begins with comprehensive data gathering from multiple sources - customer feedback, input from all the revenue teams (including Lead Generation, Presales, Sales, Revenue Operations, Solutions Consulting, Professional Services, Customer Support and Customer Success), operational metrics, and direct observation. This information must then be mapped against our three-dimensional framework to understand the true impact of each pain point.

For example, in a recent transformation project, we discovered that what appeared to be a simple issue with technical documentation was actually causing a cascade of problems across the customer journey. The revenue impact seemed modest (rated 2 out of 5), but the customer experience impact was severe (rated 5) as customers struggled to implement solutions effectively. The operational efficiency impact was also high (rated 4) as support teams spent excessive time handling preventable issues.

Leveraging Technology for Journey Optimisation

Modern journey mapping and optimisation increasingly relies on AI-powered tools and advanced analytics platforms. As discussed in the Foreword, AI has become indispensable in understanding and improving customer experiences. CRM systems enhanced with AI can predict pain points before they impact customers, while machine learning algorithms can identify patterns in customer behaviour that might be invisible to human analysis.

However, as emphasised throughout this book, technology remains an enabler rather than a solution - the fundamental work of understanding and improving the customer journey still requires human insight and strategic thinking. The key lies in combining technological capabilities with deep business understanding to create meaningful improvements in the customer experience.

Advanced analytics platforms can now process vast amounts of customer interaction data to identify patterns and potential issues before they become significant problems. AI-powered journey mapping tools can create dynamic visualisations that update in real-time as customer behaviour changes. Natural language processing can analyse customer feedback across multiple channels to identify emerging trends and sentiment shifts.

The Transformation Imperative

This systematic analysis inevitably reveals that customer journey optimisation cannot be approached piecemeal. The interconnected nature of pain points demands a holistic transformation approach. Yet this presents its own challenges, particularly in larger organisations where different departments own different parts of the journey.

I recall a particularly challenging project with a technology firm where the sales team had developed excellent processes for initial customer engagement, but the handover to implementation was consistently problematic. The sales team, measured on closed deals, had little visibility into post-sale challenges. Meanwhile, the implementation team, focused on technical metrics, didn't fully appreciate how their processes impacted customer satisfaction and renewal rates.

Breaking down these silos required more than process changes - it demanded a fundamental shift in how the organisation viewed and measured success. We established cross-functional teams responsible for end-to-end customer experience, implemented shared metrics that spanned departmental boundaries, and created feedback loops that ensured learnings from one stage of the journey informed improvements in others.

The Framework in Action

The true power of our three-dimensional framework - Revenue Impact, Customer Experience Impact, and Operational Efficiency Impact - lies in its ability to cut through complexity and prioritise actions. Consider a recent example where a client's contract approval process was causing significant delays. The initial analysis revealed:

Revenue Impact (4/5): Deals were being lost to competitors who could move more quickly, and sales cycles were extending significantly.

Customer Experience Impact (3/5): While frustrating, most customers accepted some delay as normal in enterprise purchases.

Operational Efficiency Impact (5/5): Sales teams were spending inordinate amounts of time shepherding contracts through the process, reducing their ability to pursue new opportunities.

This analysis helped build a compelling case for change, highlighting not just the immediate revenue impact but also the hidden costs in terms of sales team productivity and customer satisfaction. More importantly, it helped identify where interventions would have the most significant impact across all three dimensions.

Building Sustainable Solutions

The journey from analysis to solution requires careful consideration of both immediate fixes and long-term sustainability. In my experience, the most successful transformations balance quick wins with structural improvements. This might mean implementing temporary workarounds for the most pressing pain points while simultaneously building more comprehensive solutions.

For instance, in addressing the contract approval issues mentioned earlier, we implemented both immediate process improvements and a longer-term digital transformation initiative. The quick wins - streamlined approval hierarchies and clearer documentation requirements - delivered immediate relief. Meanwhile, the longer-term solution - a fully integrated digital contracting system - was developed and implemented in phases, ensuring sustainable improvement without disrupting ongoing business.

To ensure these improvements stick, organisations must focus on:

1. Creating robust feedback loops that continuously gather insights from all touchpoints

2. Establishing goals align across departments and with journey optimisation objectives
3. Developing clear governance structures for ongoing journey management
4. Building capabilities for continuous adaptation and improvement

Measuring Success and Maintaining Momentum

The final piece of the puzzle lies in establishing clear metrics for success. Traditional sales metrics remain important, but they must be supplemented with measures that capture the broader impact of journey improvements. To operationalise journey metrics effectively, organisations must actively track and measure:

1. Journey Stage Performance - measuring conversion rates, time spent, and satisfaction at each journey stage
2. Cross-Journey Metrics - tracking how changes in one stage impact outcomes in others
3. Customer Health Indicators - combining usage data, satisfaction scores, and engagement levels
4. Economic Impact Measures - quantifying the revenue and cost implications of journey improvements
5. Operational Efficiency Metrics - assessing internal process improvements and resource utilisation

These metrics must be integrated into regular performance reviews and governance structures outlined in Chapter 10, ensuring that customer journey optimisation remains central to transformation success. Regular assessment through the steering committee framework ensures rapid identification and response to emerging issues.

Looking Ahead

As we move into Chapter 3's exploration of solid foundations, the customer journey insights we've examined will form a crucial foundation for all subsequent transformation work. The pain points we've identified, the impacts we've measured, and the solutions we've designed must align with our ultimate goal: creating a sales engine that consistently delivers exceptional customer experiences while achieving its commercial objectives.

The frameworks introduced here - from three-dimensional impact analysis to cross-functional optimisation - provide practical tools for understanding and improving the customer journey. Combined with the systems thinking principles from Chapter 1, they enable organisations to create sustainable improvements that drive long-term sales success.

In the next chapter, we'll examine how these customer journey insights contribute to building solid foundations for transformation, ensuring our efforts remain grounded in both customer needs and organisational realities. The journey mapping and analysis frameworks we've discussed will provide essential context for this work, helping us build transformation programmes that deliver sustainable results aligned with both customer expectations and business objectives.

PART ONE | ENVISION

Chapter 3: Solid Foundations

Identification of the Problem and Need

From the change leader's perspective, the foundational stage of the turnaround journey occurs early when the pain of underperformance is first felt. It is useful to bring the underlying issues, threats, or opportunities necessitating the turnaround into sharp focus by breaking it down into the problem, evidence, and impact and this works well regardless of whether it is done internally or with outside expertise. This technique makes the case for transformative action definitive, lighting up the burning platform. It shifts discussion from speculation to substantive metrics on performance gaps demanding attention, building consensus on current weaknesses and quantifying why action must be taken now to strengthen the sales engine. Let's delve into each aspect:

1: Problem

Concisely define the core issue requiring turnaround, e.g., "Sales revenues declining for last 2 years, missing targets by 14% on average". Be specific. Creating specificity in your problem statement ensures early alignment and builds a case for change that cannot be ignored. Clearly defining core sales problems concentrates energy on measurable gaps tied to revenue and performance shortfalls, aligning stakeholders on where to direct improvement efforts for maximum, validated impact.

2: Evidence

Quantify problems with data, e.g., "14 of 20 sales regions missed 2021 targets, new customer acquisition down 20% vs. 2020 average". Facts prove this is a systematic lag requiring enterprise-level change and significant resource investment. Gather sufficient, hard-hitting evidence to ground your diagnosis in substantiated facts, revealing systematic, enterprise-level gaps over isolated dips. Seeking evidence will provide direct feedback from salespeople and collaborators on friction points, inefficiencies, poor productivity, toxic culture, leadership shortcomings, etc., giving you a strong sense of upcoming company challenges. Watch out for incomplete data creating blind spots, confirmation bias distorting fact-based evidence, and so forth. Robust feedback and data minimise blind spots on addressing true factors inhibiting sales results.

3: Impact

Document tangible consequences like "Declining market share by 7% or key customers defecting due to poor service". Impact evidence builds urgency and the business case to invest immediately to avoid worse outcomes. Understanding and quantifying the impact builds the air-tight business case for investment in sales turnaround and fuels stakeholder urgency and commitment to achieve change. Financial modelling of expected benefits from necessary investments ensures finance will be enrolled. Avoid understating or overstating projected impact without thorough evaluation and adequately quantify the promised impact. Detailing current and expected business impacts in a sufficiently quantified manner guarantees executive-level motivation to support sales changes, and gives you the best shot at aligning the buying team (coalition). Quantified impact drives and sustains focus on delivering turnaround outcomes tied directly to company profitability goals.

Benefits of Precisely Articulating the Problem

A rigorous, evidence-based definition of the current sales crisis achieves two pivotal outcomes that drive the success of the initiative:

1. Creates a Compelling Case for Immediate Action: By meticulously quantifying the financial impact of the sales crisis, an irrefutable case for urgent change is established that resonates across the organisation. The stark figures make it clear that inaction is not an option. With senior leaders aligned on the potential revenue risks, there is no room for superficial fixes or complacency. This comprehensive understanding sets a high bar, ensuring that only bold, transformative solutions are considered viable. Half-hearted measures lose their appeal against the backdrop of clearly defined challenges, reinforcing the need for decisive, large-scale action.

2. Deepens Organisational Insight and Drives Tailored Solutions: Detailed problem analysis equips the internal project team with critical insights into the root causes of organisational dysfunctions and specific pain points. This depth of understanding enables the development of customised solutions that address the unique challenges faced by the organisation. Rather than relying on generic approaches, the insights gained allow the team to craft targeted strategies that directly tackle the specific issues at hand. This positions the internal team as strategic leaders in driving change, ensuring that solutions are not only relevant but also highly effective. By defining the problem with precision, the groundwork is laid to control the direction of the initiative with authority and build a compelling case for the chosen path forward.

Overcoming Early, Inevitable Barriers

Organisational inertia, borrowed from physics, refers to the tendency of firms or institutions to persist in established patterns of behaviour, even in the face of clear signals or pressures to change. This resistance can be so powerful that even when new norms or practices are introduced, there's a gravitational pull towards the old, familiar ways. It stems from multiple sources, deeply embedded in the structure, culture, and psychological makeup of both individuals and the collective organisation.

Companies and sales engines develop complex structures and processes that provide stability and predictability. These structures, while beneficial for efficiency and coherence, can become rigid, making change implementation difficult. Layers of bureaucracy, established standard operating procedures, and sunk costs in existing systems all contribute to change resistance.

Organisational culture—the shared values, beliefs, and norms influencing how people behave within an organisation—can be a significant source of inertia. Culture shapes how employees perceive change, and a strong attachment to "the way things have always been done" can create a psychological barrier to new ideas and practices.

On an individual level, employees may resist change due to fear of the unknown, loss of control, or concern about their ability to adapt to new roles and processes. This resistance is not merely rational but deeply emotional and psychological. People find comfort and safety in familiarity, and the prospect of change can evoke anxiety and stress. The power of habit provides a sense of security and reduces the cognitive load required to make decisions. When new norms or practices are introduced, they disrupt these established habits, requiring individuals and the organisation to expend precious effort and energy to adapt. The natural human tendency to reduce discomfort and revert to familiar patterns of behaviour—habits—acts as an invisible force pulling people and teams back to its pre-existing norms.

Addressing organisational inertia requires a multifaceted approach. It involves not only changing structures and processes but also addressing the underlying cultural and psychological barriers to change. Strategies to overcome inertia must include a compelling vision for change and communicating it extensively. Involving employees in planning and implementing change helps mitigate fear and resistance, as they become active participants rather than passive recipients of change—building a sense of co-ownership. Developing skills and competencies to adopt change is crucial, fostering a culture of learning and innovation while offering the necessary support, resources, and incentives to encourage individuals to adopt new behaviours and practices. In other words, an almighty effort.

Inertia is your primary and guaranteed enemy. It is deeply rooted in often mysterious structural, cultural, and psychological factors (or human nature, to be simple). It represents a significant challenge to change initiatives, acting as an invisible force that pulls individuals and organisations back to what is familiar and comfortable. Overcoming this inertia requires something very special indeed, the absence of which accounts for so much of the change failure and wasted investments in the corporate world.

Strategies to combat inertia directly:

1. **Name it publicly and bring it to conscious awareness:** Do not allow it to be the invisible enemy that is unspoken and unseen. Forewarn people and teach everyone the signs they need to look out for and combat.

2. **Identify and empower change champions:** Cultivate respected internal voices at all levels to advocate for change. Build their brand and leverage their influence to inspire others.

3. **Highlight external threats/pressures:** External dangers like technology shifts, evolving customer demands, and increased market competition can help create urgency. Show why standing still is more perilous than changing. Create that burning platform.

4. **Celebrate small wins:** Rather than tackling everything at once, pursue incremental changes that create momentum. Ensure the success of pilot projects. Publicise successes vigorously and extensively.

5. **Challenge mental models:** Contest ingrained assumptions and shine a light on outdated or dysfunctional thinking through outside perspectives that shake things up. Bring in fresh thinking through new hires or external advisors and give them giant platforms.

6. **Make change self-reinforcing:** Build internal feedback loops and metrics-based goals so new behaviours feed on themselves. Embed changes into standard processes.

7. **Role model desired changes:** Leadership modelling new practices is more effective than just mandating new policies. People follow visible examples, and leaders MUST walk the talk.

The core principle is to employ multiple levers—vision, empowerment, external pressures, metrics alignment, new perspectives—to fundamentally shift mindsets and behaviours.

Layered, reinforcing efforts address the roots of inertia for sustainable change. Make no mistake, inertia is a formidable enemy of your cause. Treat it as such.

The Foe Called Resistance

This section might aptly be titled "Expect Problems and Prepare for a Mountain to Climb". The work of turnaround and transforming a company's sales engine can be a lot of fun, but one must expect a certain set of problems. These covert barriers exert their influences beneath the surface and in ways that would not be characterised as open or transparent. Exposing the need for change and working to implement that change, especially after exposing inefficiencies, will invariably be met with mountains of psychological resistance. These can be seen as defence mechanisms in response to perceived threats, often manifesting in predictable ways. This is especially true for senior management, who almost always fear being exposed and disrupted in how they are trying to meet their objectives and advance their careers. They silently and broodingly ask questions like, "How is this going to reveal my shortcomings and past mistakes? How will this make me look? How will this affect me, my reputation, my standing in the company? What do I stand to lose?" The list of anxieties is long, and the questions inevitable. Only leaders that are new in their role (and relatively free of baggage) welcome the prying eyes and ears of consultants doing discovery work. Most managers get fearful of being exposed and found wanting. They tend to pass this anxiety on, as scepticism or even cynicism, to their teams early on. Team members are usually quick to succumb to pressure to align with their managers' prejudices. So early on, expect outright scepticism, resistance, and even rejection of the programme, as some dig in their heels to subvert reforms that disrupt comfortable habits and power dynamics. Once the areas of dysfunction become apparent, managers point fingers at each other while refusing to acknowledge flaws on their own turf. Many teams end up hunkering down into a defensive, change-averse posture, denying even obvious problems.

Then, once the initiatives roll out, plenty of excuse-making and rationalisation emerges to explain away a lack of progress, such as lagging adoption rates. "These changes won't work here because our situation is unique," the argument goes. Individuals bend narratives to serve their interests, cherry-picking data to justify the status quo. Political infighting and jockeying run rampant.

The old guard embodying established organisational norms and cultures collide with the will of major reform – and I will be honest, it's not always clear or predictable which wins. Those leading change walk a tortuous tightrope of persuasion, alignment, transparency, and tenacity. Progress inches forward, stalls, and lurches ahead again. Eventual success and ROI are secured only through relentless determination to see the initiatives fully embedded despite the bickering, gossiping, and infighting evidenced in a blizzard of disputes, arguments, and clashes.

Rather than battering opposed voices into submission, being effective in driving change requires empathy, curiosity, consideration, and the ability to translate the change vision into relatable human terms, not rigid obligations. Progress follows an adaptive path of listening, translating, incentivising, and supporting, not brute will. Setbacks need to be framed as learning opportunities to reassess and improve rather than battles to be won. Resilience and emotional intelligence help navigate noise to uncover legitimate risks and barriers. Ultimately, major change is not secured through intimidation but inspiration. The fiercest resistance often transforms into the deepest commitment once people comprehend the vision's necessity and relevance, and when this happens, it is really rewarding.

Summary tactics to deal with covert barriers like destructive resistance:

1. **Anticipate resistance and confront it.** Go in expecting that managers will likely feel threatened, defensive, and resistant. They are human, and humans struggle with change. They take refuge in comfort zones, habits, and predictable outcomes.

Prepare mentally for scepticism, cynicism, finger-pointing, and denial of obvious problems. Don't take it personally. Above all, you must have the courage to call out the resistance—hold up a mirror, describe what you are seeing and, yes, feeling. Don't sweep it under the carpet, not even once.

2. **Build trust.** Take time to build rapport with both managers and staff. Listen sincerely to their concerns. Be transparent about the review process and what will happen with the findings. Offer and protect confidentiality.

3. **Involve stakeholders.** Get input from managers and staff on issues and goals for the project. Make them part of shaping the solutions. Give them some control in the process.

4. **Present findings tactfully, depending on your audience.** When presenting problems found to the sales organisation, use neutral, non-judgmental language. Raise issues as opportunities for improvement rather than failures or shortcomings in the teams. Be candid with the executives, or you will lose credibility.

5. **Propose solutions collaboratively. Don't be a 'know-it-all'.** Frame proposed solutions positively around business outcomes and value gained—how they will make jobs easier, improve operations, etc. Invite managers and staff to help shape solutions rather than dictating fixes.

6. **Persevere diplomatically.** Expect some continued resistance. Keep communicating and reassuring. Diplomatically stand firm on vital changes but allow input on implementation details. The key is to defuse anxiety through transparency, open dialogue, and a whole lot of tact. This can't come at the expense of structured momentum. Validate feelings but guide toward solutions. Diplomacy and perseverance are essential to overcoming overt barriers.

7. **Leverage the CEO or sponsor to help overcome resistance and barriers.** The governing idea is to proactively keep executives informed of resistance and barriers. Leverage their

authority and influence to reinforce the mandate for cooperating fully with assessment and reforms. Fear of sponsor displeasure—those with power and authority—can motivate (or compel) compliance from resistant parties. This one is so vital I will describe it in more detail:

- Brief the CEO/sponsor regularly on resistance encountered. Keep them informed on who is blocking progress and how. Let them apply pressure.

- Use the CEO's/sponsor's authority. Have them send emails directing managers to cooperate fully with the review and reforms. Stress that this is a priority.

- Arrange a kick-off meeting led by the CEO/sponsor to launch the project, convey expectations, and stress that resistance will not be tolerated.

- Have the CEO/sponsor reinforce key messages: This is happening, get on board. Frame it as an opportunity, not a threat. Non-cooperation has consequences.

Submit periodic progress reports to CEO/sponsor naming resisters. The sponsor can then have direct talks insisting on more cooperation. Fear of CEO displeasure is a surefire motivator.

PART TWO | DIAGNOSE

Chapter 4: Deep Analysis

Insights on Analysis

Deep analysis differs from identifying the problem and confirming needs (or pain points) in the initial learning stage. It's about understanding the problem at more nuanced levels and diagnosing root causes so you can build a strategy, finalise the scope of work, and create the programme plan. The goal is to thoroughly analyse the sales revenue system to identify strengths, gaps, threats, and improvement opportunities (and quick wins). In its simplest framing, it's about assessing the current state and revealing gaps across different dimensions. It must also highlight dangerous risks and advise on mitigation strategies.

Information Request

The diagnostic phase begins with an information request to obtain quantitative and qualitative data across all sales organisation areas. This gets complemented by confidential interviews with key personnel across functions like sales, marketing, product, finance, legal, and HR. The information request contains 20 categories to provide a 360-degree view of sales operations and performance.

Interviews

Structured interviews should be conducted to validate what has been learned or add nuance. Meetings should be held with sales leadership, several individual contributors, and managers from engineering, product, marketing, legal, finance, and HR teams. The goal is to gather qualitative perspectives on sales execution and identify friction points.

Output

The output is typically a report containing key findings, implications, and recommendations to address gaps and mitigate risks. Top recommendations should be ranked and include a section called quick wins. This will likely include changes to strategy, structure, processes, and sales technology. The report will form the outline for the execution roadmap.

The analysis almost always reveals the following types of gaps:

1. **Strategy:** Misalignment between the sales model and evolving customer needs or segments. Unquantified value propositions that resemble a commodity being sold might make it impossible to differentiate solutions or sell on value. Bets made on how the company will scale might be ill-conceived, based on a miscalculation of the addressable market and widespread urgency to solve a particular problem.

2. **Structures:** The current organisational structure may be misaligned to customer segments, leading to coordination issues across sales teams or shortcomings in covering key areas. Role clarity and ambiguity regarding responsibilities in newly created positions might impact decision-making and healthy collaboration.

3. **Processes:** An ad-hoc approach across the sales process might prevent operational rigour and discipline in lead management, opportunity management, and account planning. This results in inconsistent customer experiences and sales outcomes. Workflows and KPIs between collaborating functions like marketing and sales may be shoddily designed.

4. **Technology:** Sales teams might be hamstrung by a poorly integrated tech stack with no integrated visibility into customer data, insights, and forecasting analysis to effectively manage the pipeline. Current tools and systems might be disparate, requiring significant manual interventions, burning up potential productivity.

5. **Culture:** Motivation levels might vary across the sales engine, leading to attrition in key roles. Recognition mechanisms may fail to effectively reward excellence or impede collaboration and best practice sharing.

6. **Leadership:** Sales leaders may be winging it with inadequate skills and tools to effectively coach frontline teams and foster talent. Their own capability gaps around value or consultative

solution selling may prevent them from leading from the front or knowing which gaps to coach.

7. **Capability:** The company might require advanced consultative selling capabilities in specific industry verticals, for example, capital markets, where a lack of depth of experience is painfully notable. You might find skill gaps in conducting value selling conversations aligned to business outcomes due to lacking commercial acumen. Commonly, one finds limited capability in value realisation practices to grasp and deliver ROI.

8. **Talent Management:** The organisation might have difficulty hiring the right talent or retaining their best salespeople once they have matured into solid, consistent performers. The company might find it impossible to compete with key competitors for the best and brightest graduates because its employee value proposition might be poor.

Root Cause Analysis

A crucial, confrontational, and always-controversial component of the diagnostic stage is root cause analysis. Simply identifying performance gaps risks solving symptoms rather than the underlying disease. Probe above and beyond the surface down to the fundamental drivers impacting sales outcomes. Using the trusted old iceberg metaphor, assume that everything above the surface is written down somewhere—documented, catalogued, and accessible—be that policies, agreements, delineations of responsibilities, and so forth. The stuff under the surface is not always obvious and for which no consensus can be found—political factions, power dynamics, antagonistic relationships, and so forth.

For example, declining average deal sizes may signal issues with value-based selling capability. However, further analysis may reveal the root cause as a narrow solution set unable to address evolving customer needs. Or churn in critical roles could indicate motivational issues but, upon deeper reflection, point to inadequate hiring profiles and onboarding, or a toxic leader killing morale and cohesion.

Getting to root causes requires moving beyond obvious culprits to consider interdependencies across change dimensions. Leveraging organisational network analysis, process mapping exercises, and statistical analysis has equipped me to triangulate high impact, yet not so obvious, root causes. These then become the cornerstones in constructing the turnaround roadmap.

Grappling with root causes almost always implies more complex, longer-term solutions. However, lasting turnaround cannot occur by simply addressing surface issues. Committing to root cause diagnosis, while challenging, provides the blueprint for targeted strategies that deliver material, sustainable improvements.

Documenting and Structuring Findings

After an exhaustive diagnostic process, tensions run high as stakeholders anxiously await the findings. Many brace for criticism, and most are desperate to eliminate the uncertainty that comes with not knowing while gaining clarity on the path forward.

When presenting findings, balance brutal honesty with hope and inspirational vision. The centrepiece of the report must always be the executive summary conveying overarching themes, followed by detailed findings, implications, and recommendations by turnaround dimension (strategy, structures, processes, etc.).

For example, the diagnosis may reveal misaligned organisational structures hampering customer-centricity. The findings would capture specifics around disjointed coverage, key account coordination failures, and disjointed solutions. Implications could highlight rising customer churn, declining share of wallet, and inferior competitive win rates. Finally, the recommendations would propose structural realignment options, integration mechanisms, and revised role clarity.

Similarly, capability gaps around consultative value selling would list specific shortcomings in discovery, value articulation, and ROI measurement as findings. Implications would project lower deal values, compressed margins, and commoditisation threats.

Recommendations would then detail capability programmes, specialist hiring, and presales augmentation.

Always include a distinct section on quick wins showcasing some early victory potential to build momentum while constructively destabilising the status quo. Highlighting tangible initiatives resonating symbolically catalyses appetite for bolder interventions. While sobering and scary, thoughtful findings presentation provides the roadmap, laying foundations for aligned understanding of current inadequacies while painting an optimistic picture of a transformed future state.

Finessing the Presentation of Findings

Navigating the crucial findings presentation requires finesse and advanced planning. Rather than broadly circulating the report initially, you must schedule preview meetings with key leaders and sponsors. This provides a forum for aligning on reactions and calibrating responses. It allows pre-emptively addressing areas of expected contention while planning for pushback. Sponsors can be powerful allies in disseminating and reinforcing key insights. For example, an impending restructure recommendation could be emotionally charged, even explosive. Sharing this strategic logic and options with affected leaders ahead of time allows answering outstanding questions and objections. It also equips them to cascade direction to their teams during the official presentation.

Similar previews for leaders accountable for sales capability building allow expectation setting on the realities of skill gaps. Rather than reacting defensively, they stand a better chance of becoming active co-creators of improvement roadmaps. These pre-emptive alignments limit surprise, confusion, and knee-jerk responses. They equip leadership with narratives to convey the rationale to their teams. Selective previews protect people and enable containment planning to accelerate informed acceptance. This upholds the credibility of recommendations while activating sponsors as active heralds across the organisation. The trust established primes conditions necessary for cooperative design of the impending turnaround.

Programme Scope Refinement and Adjustment

You still have not designed the turnaround programme and done the planning, but here you will need to do a quick calibration. Here is one example of the certainty that the stages are not perfectly linear. Your analysis will have not only ruffled many a feather but unearthed (forgive the jargon) low-hanging fruit and the opportunity for quick wins (that you highlighted in the report). After the initial current state assessment, you'll need recalibration based on what you have learned and to set the right expectations on turnaround depth versus available bandwidth/willingness to absorb change. Areas evaluated as needing improvement—like sales strategy or value propositions—may require a feedback plan, especially around expected pushback. Quick wins should be directed at low-controversy, high-impact areas like enhanced sales analytics or automated performance dashboards that can demonstrate results fast. Getting the scope right upfront directly serves sales' interest as well. Overpromising massive overnight change risks disappointment and eroded credibility. However, selling a journey focused squarely on mutually understood priorities aligned to client readiness can build trust in attainable outcomes.

Securing Quick Wins

There is often significant pressure to identify and deliver quick wins during the early stages of a turnaround, even before the programme has been designed in full, let alone piloted. The expression of low-hanging fruit always comes up, and leaders understandably don't want to lose the opportunity for quick and painless remedies that can boost momentum and morale.

Essentially, this upfront refinement and quick win targeting boosts the alliance between consultant and client against the looming barriers. It sets realistic expectations while proactively building confidence in anticipated positive outcomes—crucial to retaining executive sponsorship over the turnaround marathon.

The pressure to demonstrate tangible progress early in a sales turnaround journey cannot be underestimated. After an extensive audit has revealed gaps across the sales organisation, expectations run high. Delivering early gains artfully balances pragmatism while signalling turnaround intent and competence. Too small or incremental, and they risk dismissal as window dressing. Too ambitious or disruptive, and organisational antibodies swiftly neutralise the intervention. Quick wins are strategically designed to resonate symbolically, boosting internal sponsors' visibility while pragmatically advancing key metrics. For example, a new dashboard highlighting metrics that lead to stagnant account growth can light a fire under the account management function while paving the way for instilling data-driven decision-making and could even kickstart a culture shift towards greater transparency and accountability.

Avoid the temptation to overengineer quick wins or mistake mere activity for meaningful impact. Instead, prioritise simple, sustainable, and scalable improvements that are directly aligned with the turnaround objectives, keeping the focus firmly on enhancing sales performance. Implement these quick wins effectively and communicate them widely to generate early momentum. Each successive quick win helps to shift scepticism into a growing appetite for more significant change. Rather than being superficial fixes, a strategically planned sequence of quick wins serves to disrupt the status quo in a constructive way, setting the stage for a broader transformation. Ultimately, quick wins should deliver clear, measurable impact while preparing the organisation for the longer journey of sustained improvement.

Principles for quick wins:

Laser Focus

Maintain ruthless prioritisation on 1-2 initial quick wins with the highest turnaround symbolism and measurable sales impact. Attempting too many dilutes focus and strains bandwidth.

Leverage Existing Momentum

Identify initiatives already underway aligned to turnaround goals and accelerate or enhance them for quick win designation. This avoids reinventing the wheel.

Draft Implementation Plans

Define clear accountabilities, timelines, resource needs, risks, and mitigation steps as an executable roadmap for each quick win. This equips those responsible and ultimately accountable to rapidly deliver.

Appoint Best Performance

Assign top talents as champions and contributors on quick win teams. This infuses initiatives with urgency, expertise, and excellence in execution. Vitally, it also reduces risk at this critical juncture.

Showcase Synergies

I am trying to resurrect the most ubiquitous corporate word of my generation because it really is unparalleled. But I digress. Spotlight how singular quick wins have ripple effects across turnaround goals like data-driven decision-making, capability building, and process improvement.

Amplify through Communications

Socialise and publicise quick wins extensively. This continually spotlights turnaround motion and builds engagement.

Ingrain as Habit

Operationalise quick wins into rhythms like weekly or quarterly performance or business reviews and frontline manager coaching. This drives adoption and sustainability.

PART TWO | DIAGNOSE

Chapter 5: Dimensions of
Performance and Change

1. Strategy

Insights on Strategy

In our fast-paced business world, even the best sales strategies need regular tweaking to stay relevant and effective. Sales strategy is the guiding light for go-to-market success, especially in an age where buyers self-educate and make decisions committee-style. With business environments in flux, sales strategy must stay dynamic, adapting swiftly based on market signals and customer needs.

The sales strategy is as fundamental a factor of success as any. Oddly, this highly complex dimension can be hotly debated, late into a company's life and long after product market fit and successful scaling. Questions like "are we selling the right products in the right markets?" and "do we have the best channels to market?" can rage into debate at multiple junctures during the Turnaround. I've learned the only viable way to resolve endless strategy debates is to have data, derived from credible study and analysis, on your side. But more on that later.

Obviously, at the heart of any successful sales turnaround lies a clear, adaptive sales strategy that aligns with broader business goals while targeting the most valuable markets, segments, and accounts. Sales strategy forms the backbone of go-to-market plans, guiding critical decisions around coverage models, skill development, incentives, and sales and marketing integration. Leading organisations incorporate both quantitative and qualitative insights across these areas to craft differentiated, insight-led strategies that fuel growth.

The sales strategy is the action plan specifying how an organisation will reach target customers and achieve competitive advantage. It covers all aspects of bringing a product or service to market, including positioning, segmentation, channels, customer journey mapping, pricing, and marketing. The sales strategy aligns product development, marketing, sales, and customer support to ensure a unified approach, aiming to deliver value, meet objectives, and drive sustainable growth.

The dynamic nature of markets, customer preferences, and competitive landscapes necessitates ongoing optimisation of the sales strategy to ensure it remains aligned with changing conditions and new opportunities.

The sales strategy's success hinges on seamless collaboration among sales, marketing, customer success, product, and presales teams. This ensures consistent understanding of target segments, value propositions, support mechanisms, product trajectories, and the technical evaluations critical during the sales process.

Hallmarks of Sales Strategy Excellence

1. **Systematic Innovation Integration:** Integrating customer and market-driven innovation into offerings ensures the organisation stays competitive and relevant.

2. **Competitive Differentiation and Value Proposition Clarity:** Clearly articulating competitive differentiators and value propositions is key.

3. **Strategic Customer Segmentation and Targeting:** Advanced segmentation and targeting strategies leverage data analytics to identify high-value segments and tailor efforts.

4. **Collaborative Strategic Planning and Execution:** The best sales strategies are co-created with various departments to ensure a unified approach.

5. **Dynamic Route-to-Market Strategies:** Flexibility to adapt route-to-market strategies based on evolving conditions is crucial.

6. **Strategic Alignment with Corporate Vision and Culture:** Aligning sales strategies with corporate goals, vision and culture builds a sustainable, values-driven brand.

7. **Proactive Risk Management and Ethical Selling:** Incorporating proactive risk management and ethical selling builds trust with customers and stakeholders.

Assessing Sales Strategy

Assessing sales strategy requires understanding its centrality to the organisation's identity and the sensitivity it holds for leadership. The sales strategy isn't merely a business component but the linchpin securing the organisation's competitive position. It reflects the ethos, aspirations, and commitment to delivering customer value.

The sales strategy embodies the tactical response to market dynamics, competitive pressures, and customer needs. It charts the organisation's future, making the stakes high. Leaders, as custodians of the strategic vision, often view sales strategy as an extension of their leadership efficacy and professional legacy. Thus, discourse around sales strategy carries personal investment and emotional engagement from leadership. Caution is warranted: assessing and recalibrating sales strategy must be approached with discretion, sensitivity, and awareness of implications.

Assessing a sales strategy requires a dual lens: one recognising strategic imperatives, another appreciating the human element in strategic formulation and execution. Navigate these enquiries balancing analytical rigour and empathetic engagement.

1: Revenue Growth and Market Share
How have revenue growth and market share changed as a result of the sales strategy?

Assessing revenue growth and market share directly measures the sales strategy's effectiveness in expanding the business and capturing market share. These metrics reflect the ability to convert strategy into tangible financial success and competitive advantage.

2: Customer Acquisition and Retention Rates
What impact has the sales strategy had on customer acquisition and retention rates?

The effectiveness of a sales strategy is evident in its ability to attract new customers and retain existing ones. High acquisition rates indicate successful market penetration; strong retention rates suggest the strategy fosters customer loyalty and satisfaction.

3: Return on Sales Investment

What is the ROI for sales initiatives under the current strategy?

Evaluating sales initiatives' ROI offers insights into the financial efficiency of the sales strategy. This analysis identifies investments yielding the highest returns, guiding resource allocation and strategic adjustments to maximise profitability. If a company has no clue, it's evidence of a lack of maturity.

4: Customer Lifetime Value

How does the sales strategy impact CLV?

CLV estimates the total revenue expected from a single customer account. An effective sales strategy should focus on, and have a history of, maximising CLV through upselling, cross-selling, and enhancing satisfaction to foster long-term loyalty.

5: Innovation and Adaptability

How effectively does the organisation integrate customer and market-driven innovation into its offerings?

Innovation and adaptability are essential for maintaining competitiveness. This involves systematically incorporating feedback and market trends into offerings, ensuring the organisation remains relevant and ahead of market demands.

6: Competitive Differentiation

Is there a clear articulation of competitive differentiators vividly described in marketing collateral and value propositions?

Clarity of competitive differentiators and value propositions is vital. It enables effectively communicating why solutions are superior, ensuring advantages are consistently conveyed in all sales and marketing efforts.

7: Customer Segmentation and Targeting

Does the organisation employ advanced segmentation and targeting strategies?

Effective segmentation and targeting maximise efficiency and impact by focusing on the most valuable markets and segments.

This approach leverages data analytics for deep insights, allowing customised strategies.

8: Collaborative Strategic Planning
To what extent are sales strategies co-created with various departments?

Co-creating sales strategies with Product, Marketing, Finance, and Customer Success ensures a unified approach. This collaborative process fosters alignment, enhancing the ability to meet expectations and achieve objectives.

9: Ethical Selling and Risk Management
How are ethical selling and risk management incorporated within the sales strategy?

Ethical selling and proactive risk management are foundational for building trust. Incorporating guidelines for ethical conduct and risk mitigation ensures integrity and sustainability.

10: Strategic Foundation and Validation
How is the sales strategy validated against market research, prioritising delivering value over showcasing features?

A mature sales strategy is built on validated customer needs and market dynamics, prioritising delivering value over features. Validation through research demonstrates commitment to data-driven decisions, ensuring alignment with market needs and expectations. While intuition and experience shape strategy, a mature approach recognises the importance of balancing these with empirical evidence.

2. Structure

Insights on Structure

Exploring the relationship between structure and performance, productivity, and efficiency within a revenue organisation can be a complex task, but the insights gained are invaluable. Through my years of experience, I've discovered that focusing on interdependencies rather than strict hierarchies can foster a more agile, adaptive, and high-performing culture. By decentralising decision-making and empowering employees at all levels, organisations can enhance responsiveness, accelerate operational pace, and boost engagement and satisfaction. Moreover, tailoring organisational structures to fit the unique demands of different markets can lead to optimised resource allocation and sharper competitive advantages. Leveraging data analytics to inform structural changes helps identify inefficiencies and areas for improvement, resulting in a more finely tuned operation. Lastly, adopting fluid and dynamic role definitions encourages an entrepreneurial mindset, driving innovation and continuous improvement in processes and outcomes. By incorporating these insights, revenue organisations can develop a more sophisticated understanding of how structure influences performance, productivity, and efficiency, ultimately leading to greater success in today's fast-paced business landscape.

Transforming sales structures aligns four key domains:

1. **Strategic Orientation:** Structures facilitate strategic plays – market expansion, vertical penetration, solution focus, or channel shifts.

2. **Customer Alignment:** Coverage maps to targeted customer profiles, with generalist/specialist models varying by type.

3. **Operational Efficiency:** Non-sales support lifts administrative burdens. Enablement resources plug skill and content gaps.

4. **Adaptable Design:** Dynamic "networked" models trump static structures. Competency clusters assemble flexibly for evolving needs.

Hallmarks of Sales Structure Excellence

1. **Integrated Cross-Functional Collaboration:** Seamless integration with marketing, product, and customer success teams for unified experiences and outcomes. The structure promotes smooth collaboration, enabling the development of cohesive strategies and the delivery of consistent customer experiences.

2. **Dynamic Adaptability and Market Responsiveness:** The structure proactively evolves with market changes, customer feedback, and competitive pressures, facilitating rapid pivots into actionable tactics. It accommodates changes in market conditions, customer needs, and technological advancements, determining the organisation's resilience and long-term success.

3. **Comprehensive Role Clarity and Specialisation:** Clearly defined roles aligned with segments and markets, optimising the level of specialisation. Role evolution keeps pace with trends and growth, ensuring the sales team remains agile and effective.

4. **Scalable and Efficient Infrastructure:** Robust technology, data, and automation enhance productivity and scalability. The structure leverages these tools to streamline processes, improve efficiency, and support the sales team's ability to drive revenue growth.

5. **Strategic Alignment with Organisational Goals:** The sales structure is intimately aligned with the company's vision, goals, and values, fostering unity and purpose. It ensures coherence between the sales team's objectives and the overarching strategic direction of the organisation.

6. **Data-Driven Decisions and Metrics:** Clear, relevant metrics guide strategy, operations, and individual performance, ensuring accountability and continuous improvement. The structure facilitates data-driven decision-making, enabling the sales team to adapt and optimise their approach based on insights.

7. **Empowered and Engaged Sales Force:** The structure provides autonomy, resources, and support for the sales team to innovate and excel. Salespeople are actively involved in shaping strategies and tactics, fostering a sense of ownership and engagement.

8. **Customer-Centric Design:** The sales structure prioritises customer needs and experiences in organisational and operational models. It enables targeted coverage of key segments and markets, reflecting the organisation's ability to understand, segment the market, and tailor strategies for diverse customer needs.

9. **Sustainable Growth:** The structure promotes enduring practices and a focus on building long-term trust and success with customers. It balances short-term objectives with the need for sustainable, mutually beneficial relationships.

10. **Resilience and Proactive Risk Management:** The sales structure anticipates, manages, and mitigates risks, adapting to external pressures. It is designed to be resilient, enabling the sales team to navigate challenges and maintain performance in the face of adversity.

Assessing Sales Structures

Reconfiguring sales structure carries profound human and operational implications. Balancing strategic goals with these aspects is key. Clear communication, inclusive decisions, and support mechanisms facilitate smooth transitions while respecting dignity and aspirations.

1: Integrated Cross-Functional Collaboration
How does the structure promote seamless integration and collaboration with marketing, product, and customer success teams for unified experiences and outcomes?

This evaluates the structure's ability to enable smooth collaboration across functions, facilitating the development of cohesive strategies and consistent customer experiences.

2: Dynamic Adaptability and Market Responsiveness
How does the structure proactively evolve with market changes, customer feedback, and competitive pressures, enabling rapid pivots into actionable tactics?

This assesses the structure's capacity to accommodate changes in market conditions, customer needs, and technological advancements, determining the organisation's resilience and long-term success.

3: Comprehensive Role Clarity and Specialisation
Are roles clearly defined and aligned with segments and markets, optimising the level of specialisation?

This examines whether the structure provides role clarity and enables role evolution to keep pace with trends and growth, ensuring the sales team remains agile and effective.

4: Scalable and Efficient Infrastructure
Does the structure leverage robust technology, data, and automation to enhance productivity and scalability?

This evaluates how the structure utilises tools to streamline processes, improve efficiency, and support the sales team's ability to drive revenue growth.

5: Strategic Alignment with Organisational Goals
Is the sales structure intimately aligned with the company's vision, goals, and values, fostering unity and purpose?

This assesses the coherence between the sales team's objectives and the overarching strategic direction of the organisation.

6: Data-Driven Decisions and Metrics
How does the structure facilitate data-driven decision-making, with clear, relevant metrics guiding strategy, operations, and individual performance?

This examines the structure's ability to ensure accountability and continuous improvement by enabling the sales team to adapt and optimise their approach based on insights.

7: Empowered and Engaged Sales Force

Does the structure provide autonomy, resources, and support for the sales team to innovate and excel, actively involving them in shaping strategies and tactics?

This evaluates the structure's capacity to foster a sense of ownership and engagement among salespeople.

8: Customer-Centric Design

How does the sales structure prioritise customer needs and experiences in organisational and operational models, enabling targeted coverage of key segments and markets?

This assesses the structure's ability to understand, segment the market, and tailor strategies for diverse customer needs.

9: Sustainable Growth

Does the structure promote enduring practices and a focus on building long-term trust and success with customers, balancing short-term objectives with sustainable relationships?

This examines the structure's emphasis on fostering mutually beneficial, long-lasting customer relationships.

10: Resilience and Proactive Risk Management

How does the sales structure anticipate, manage, and mitigate risks, adapting to external pressures to maintain performance in the face of adversity?

This evaluates the structure's resilience and ability to navigate challenges effectively.

3. Processes

Insights on Processes

Optimising sales processes is key to achieving the best results, just like precision in Formula 1 pit stops is crucial to winning races. The opportunity blueprint exemplifies why process optimisation is critical, outlining the entire process for moving deals forward, bringing clarity, consistency, and discipline to the team. It serves as the foundation for effective opportunity management, ensuring smooth lead handoff, regular pipeline reviews, efficient problem-solving for stalled deals, and faster sales cycles.

Viewing processes through a systems thinking lens provides valuable insights into how operational workflows and methodologies interact and impact the overall sales revenue engine. This perspective helps identify leverage points for improvement and innovation. For instance, prospecting is not just the initial step; it's the entry point into the sales system. Modifying how teams engage with potential customers through integrated marketing initiatives can significantly influence the quality of leads entering the system.

Streamlining sales processes requires acknowledging the interdependencies and feedback loops within the sales system. By designing processes to reduce sales cycle times, improve effectiveness, and enhance customer satisfaction, organisations can create resilient, adaptable, and effective sales systems that drive superior performance and customer alignment.

Hallmarks of High-Performance and Efficient Sales Processes

1. **Streamlined and Personalised Sales Motions:** Optimised to reduce unnecessary efforts and streamline interactions. Tailoring communication and solutions to meet specific needs and pain points.

2. **Clear Definition and Segmentation of Target Market:** Focused on prospects with the highest potential for conversion.

Designed around customer and market segmentation, with dedicated teams specialising in specific areas.

3. **Structured Sales Pipeline Management:** Effective management with clear stages and criteria for progression. Consistent and effective follow-up to ensure no opportunities are lost.

4. **Data-Driven Decision Making and Performance Monitoring:** Utilising data analytics to inform strategies and decisions. Regular monitoring and analysis for timely adjustments and optimisation.

5. **Automated Administrative Tasks and Effective Use of CRM Systems:** Freeing up salespeople to focus on selling and building relationships. Leveraging systems to track interactions, manage contacts, and analyse data.

6. **Integration of Sales, Marketing, and Other Functions:** Close alignment for consistent messaging and equipping sales teams. Fostering collaboration and cross-functional teamwork.

7. **Agility, Flexibility, and Adaptability:** Adapting strategies and processes in response to market changes and customer feedback. Enabling quick responses to changing market conditions and customer needs.

8. **Customer Feedback Loop:** Incorporating feedback for continuous improvement. Maintaining a focus on enhancing customer satisfaction and loyalty.

9. **Collaborative Sales Execution:** Fostering collaboration and cross-functional teamwork. Ensuring smooth lead handoff and efficient problem-solving for stalled deals.

10. **Continuous Process Optimisation:** Regularly evaluating and optimising processes to reduce sales cycle times and improve effectiveness. Ensuring alignment with the evolving needs of customers and the dynamic business landscape.

By consolidating these hallmarks, organisations can focus on the most critical aspects of high-performance and efficient sales processes while still maintaining a comprehensive approach to optimising their sales engine for revenue growth and customer satisfaction.

Assessing Sales Processes

The allure of modifying inept processes to enhance efficiency, speed, and performance is undeniable. However, changes to one process invariably ripple out and can affect others, often far removed. This interconnectedness demands a cautious and holistic evaluation of potential changes. Improvement in one area can inadvertently introduce inefficiencies in another.

1: Streamlined Sales Motions
How are sales motions optimised to enhance efficiency and speed for both the sales team and the client?

Streamlining involves eliminating unnecessary steps and simplifying interactions to make the process faster and more efficient. Being easy to buy from is imperative in today's age.

2: Target Market Definition
How well-defined is the target market to focus sales efforts on the highest value potential prospects?

A clear definition ensures that efforts are concentrated on prospects most likely to convert at the highest value, improving both efficiency and effectiveness.

3: Structured Sales Pipeline Management
Are there any barriers to efficient lead nurturing and progression in the pipeline?

Effective pipeline management, with clear stages and criteria, is crucial for moving leads through efficiently. Sales velocity depends on it. This question looks for barriers to smooth lead qualification, nurturing, and progressing.

4: Data-Driven Decision Making
In what ways does the organisation utilise data analytics within its sales processes to inform strategies and decisions?

Leveraging data analytics ensures better decisions and efforts directed towards the most fruitful and high potential opportunities.

5: Automated Administrative Tasks
How are administrative tasks automated to allow salespeople to focus more on selling and relationship-building?

The best performing organisations maximise selling time and minimise administration burdens. Automation frees up valuable time for salespeople to engage directly with prospects and do more actual selling.

6: Personalised Customer Engagement
How are communication, insight, and solution offerings personalised for each prospect to enhance sales effectiveness?

Tailoring to the specific needs and pain points of each prospect significantly increases the effectiveness of sales efforts and improves conversion rates.

7: Consistent and Effective Follow-Up
What systematic approach is employed to ensure consistent and effective follow-up with prospects?

A structured follow-up process is essential to maintain engagement and advance prospects through the sales funnel. This question delves into the rigour around follow-up, evaluating how these practices help in capturing opportunities and keeping prospects engaged.

8: Integration of Sales, Marketing, and Other Functions
How integrated are sales with marketing and other collaborative functions to ensure cohesive customer engagement?

Close alignment and integration are crucial for delivering consistent messaging and equipping sales teams with the necessary tools and information. This question assesses the level of cross-functional collaboration and its effectiveness in supporting sales activities, as well as cross or upselling.

9: Effective Process Adherence through the Use of CRM Systems

How are CRM systems configured to bring rigour to processes and organise sales efforts and utilise customer insights?

Effective configuration and use of CRM systems are pivotal for tracking interactions, managing contacts, and analysing customer data. It enables processes to be a source of efficiency rather than a leak in productivity.

10: The Combination of Discipline, Agility, and Flexibility in Sales Processes

How do sales processes demonstrate disciplined execution while maintaining agility and flexibility in response to market changes and customer feedback?

The ability to adapt sales strategies and processes is essential for maintaining relevance and effectiveness. However, operational rigour and process discipline are critical, and getting the balance right is vital.

4. Technology and Tooling

Insights on Technology and Tooling

Several technology trends now shape the competitive landscape for ambitious sales leaders. Intelligent CRM platforms use AI and machine learning to prescribe content sequencing, highlight expansion potential, and trigger automated campaigns based on customer signals. Sales enablement has gone mobile and digital, making training, coaching, and content sharing dynamic and personalised. On-demand resources boost readiness for customer conversations. Automation is everywhere, with AI bots scheduling meetings, nurturing prospects, and updating records, elevating human productivity. Seamless tech-human handoffs across sales process stages will only accelerate. Advances in analytics, AI, and automation have expanded possibilities across sales workflows—from optimising lead routing to predicting deal conversion and personalising buyer experiences. But in the world of B2B enterprise sales, the CRM is the centre of the tech stack and the most important to me. I distinguish it from other tooling, although many can, and should, live inside the CRM.

Hallmarks of Technology and Tooling Excellence

1. **Buyer Alignment:** Excellence is achieved when technology tools are precisely mapped to every stage of the customer's journey, enhancing how customers engage, educate themselves, and make decisions. This includes leveraging AI for content personalisation, optimising campaign performance, and ensuring the tech stack supports dynamic personalisation at the individual level.

2. **User Adoption:** Adoption hinges on selecting tools that simplify sales activities and are intuitive to use. This involves prioritising technologies that offer virtual assistance, predictive opportunity analytics, and AI-powered recommendations, making daily sales tasks more manageable and efficient.

3. **Integration Synergies:** A high-functioning tech stack requires seamless integration between its components, enabling data

sharing and comprehensive insights. Technologies should facilitate a unified view of the customer journey, integrating marketing, sales, and customer success data to provide a holistic understanding of customer interactions.

4. **Results Alignment:** Continuous evaluation of technology investments against their anticipated benefits is crucial. This involves assessing whether tools like predictive lead scoring, AI-enhanced content creation, and automated marketing operations deliver on their promise to improve productivity, efficiency, and revenue.

5. **Executive Leadership:** Active engagement from executive leadership in the selection and use of sales tools underscores the importance of technology in driving sales success. Leadership should champion the adoption of mobile-first tools, agile deployment practices, and ensure that sales operations teams are equipped to support technology implementation and adoption.

6. **Mobile-First Approach:** Emphasising cloud-based tools with strong mobile capabilities ensures that sales teams can access critical information and engage with customers anytime, anywhere, promoting flexibility and responsiveness.

7. **Agile Deployment:** Incorporating continuous feedback from users to iteratively enhance tool features and functionality ensures that the technology remains relevant and effective. This agile approach to technology deployment keeps the sales process adaptive to changing market demands and customer needs.

8. **Impact Metrics:** Utilising detailed metrics to evaluate the impact of technology on sales performance and customer experience is essential. This includes analysing how tools affect sales cycle times, customer engagement levels, and overall sales effectiveness.

In the landscape of sales turnaround, the integration of technology and tooling emerges as an inevitable and indispensable workstream.

This necessity is rooted in the fundamental requirement to construct or modify critical sales processes and tools, such as the Opportunity Management Blueprint, ensuring their seamless integration within the Customer Relationship Management (CRM) system.

Technology broadly encompasses the digital infrastructure and platforms that underpin sales operations, including CRM systems that house the sales process. It provides the foundational systems necessary for the operation and management of sales activities.

Tooling, on the other hand, refers to the specific templates, frameworks, new applications, and sales enablement resources—such as battlecards and pitch decks—designed to directly augment the sales process. Tooling represents the practical application of technology, offering tangible assets and resources that sales teams interact with daily to enhance sales tactics and strategies. I know that this workstream is inevitable. For one, the CRM system, pivotal in modern sales operations, necessitates the integration of both technology and tooling to support the sales process effectively. As organisations evolve, the need to refine or introduce new processes and tools becomes imperative, demanding their incorporation within the CRM to ensure they are actionable, trackable, and scalable.

Furthermore, the inherent dynamism of sales processes requires frequent adjustments, making the agility provided by technology and tooling essential. This workstream ensures continuous updates to reflect the latest strategies, processes, and best practices, stemming from the ongoing need for evolution and technological adaptation.

Effective sales operations depend on the seamless integration of technologies and the sharing of data across functions. The technology and tooling workstream facilitates this integration, ensuring that changes in tools and processes are reflected across the entire technology stack, enabling comprehensive analytics and integrated workflows.

Organisational turnarounds demand clear visibility into performance metrics and sales outcomes. Modifications or creations of tools and processes must be mirrored in the CRM and other technologies, providing leadership with the insights needed for informed decision-making and maintaining strategic alignment.

The success of new or modified tools and processes hinges on their adoption by the sales team. This workstream plays a crucial role in facilitating adoption, ensuring intuitive integration into the CRM system, and supported by training and change management initiatives.

Tooling's integration into the tech stack is vital for enhancing sales processes and enablement. It addresses immediate sales team needs, providing the necessary resources for effective customer engagement. The development and deployment of tooling are often directly tied to sales enablement initiatives, requiring regular updates to reflect changes in sales methodology and customer engagement strategies. This continuous adaptation and the user-centric design of tooling are essential for driving efficiency, effectiveness, and innovation in the sales process.

Assessing Technology and Tooling

There is a kind of dichotomy between the aspirations of sales professionals and the strategic objectives of management regarding technology and tooling in sales organisations, and it encapsulates an awkward tension that must be navigated with some awareness and even finesse. On one hand, sales teams want to sell with minimal burden and time wastage. This leads them to often express frustration with over-engineered technology and tools. Their critique frequently centres on the perception that such systems serve more to satisfy managerial metrics than to genuinely facilitate the sales process. Any tool that does not directly contribute to closing deals or easing the sales motion is viewed with scepticism, if not outright disdain.

Contrastingly, from the management perspective, the deployment of sophisticated technology and tooling is not a mere exercise in data collection or an attempt to impose oversight, but a strategic imperative aimed at driving productivity and extracting actionable insights from quality data inputs. This is about securing a competitive edge in the marketplace. Navigating this tension effectively is vital for fostering an environment where technology serves as a catalyst for sales excellence, rather than a source of contention.

1: Buyer Alignment with Technology

How well are the technology and tools aligned with each stage of the customer's journey, enhancing engagement, education, and decision-making processes?

The better the tech and tools are calibrated to the buyer's journey, the more effective they will be in achieving desired outcomes. Assessing buyer alignment involves examining how technology supports customer engagement strategies, facilitates educational content delivery, and aids in the decision-making process. This now includes leveraging AI for content personalisation and optimising campaign performance to improve the overall customer experience.

2: User Adoption of Sales Tools

Are the tech and tools used consistently? What strategies are in place to ensure high user adoption?

Evaluating user adoption shines a light on how much value is gained from using what is available and mandated. Prioritising configuration that really works and adds value to both users and managers is key. Tools that offer real assistance and add tangible benefits encourage regular use and integration into daily workflows.

3: Integration Synergies Across the Tech Stack

How seamlessly integrated are the components of the tech stack, enabling comprehensive insights and data sharing?

Assessing integration synergies involves examining the interoperability of technologies, data flow between systems, and the extent to which these integrations contribute to execution efficiency and a cohesive understanding of the sales process and customer engagement.

4: Continuous Evaluation of Technology

How and when are technology investments evaluated against their anticipated benefits in improving productivity, efficiency, and revenue?

This involves analysing performance metrics, user feedback, and ROI to ensure that technology investments are meeting or exceeding expected outcomes, particularly in areas like predictive lead scoring and AI-enhanced content creation.

5: Executive Leadership in Technology Selection and Use

How engaged are executive leaders in the selection, implementation, and adoption of sales technologies? Do they personally lead from the front in adoption?

Assessing executive leadership involvement includes looking at their adoption, decision-making processes, investment priorities, and how leadership advocates for and supports technology use within the sales organisation. If sales leaders and team managers don't lead the way in adoption, team members will develop indifference around adoption and resent being held to account on issues like data quality in the CRM.

6: Emphasis on Mobile-First Technology

How does the organisation prioritise cloud-based tools with strong mobile capabilities to ensure sales team flexibility and responsiveness?

Evaluating the emphasis on mobile-first technology involves assessing the availability and functionality of mobile applications, remote access capabilities, and how these tools support sales activities outside the traditional office environment and when in front of the customer.

7: Agile Deployment and Continuous Feedback from Users

How is continuous feedback from users incorporated to iteratively enhance tool features and functionality? Are cries for improvements or modifications listened to and acted upon, or perpetually ignored?

Assessing agile deployment involves looking at mechanisms for collecting user feedback, the process for implementing changes based on this feedback, and how quickly and effectively the organisation can iterate on technology features to ensure sellers have the best tech and tools available and don't envy the competitions.

8: Impact Metrics for Technology Evaluation

What detailed metrics are used to evaluate the impact of technology on sales performance and customer experience?

This includes analysing how tools affect sales velocity and overall sales effectiveness, examining the data collected, and how insights derived from these metrics inform strategic decisions, process improvements, and additional investments.

9: Technology Support for Selling to Buying Coalitions

How do sales technologies and tools facilitate engagement with buying coalitions that have diverse agendas, needs, and priorities?

Selling to buying coalitions requires understanding and addressing a variety of stakeholder needs and priorities. This question assesses how sales technologies, such as CRM systems and AI-driven analytics, support the sales team's ability to segment and personalise engagement strategies for different members of the buying coalition. It involves evaluating tools for their capability to provide insights into individual stakeholder preferences, track multi-threaded conversations, and tailor communication to address the specific concerns and interests of each coalition member, thereby enhancing the effectiveness of sales efforts across varied agendas.

10: Technology-Driven Reduction of Sales Friction

In what ways do sales technologies contribute to, or detract from, the elimination of friction points in the sales process, thereby accelerating sales velocity?

The reduction of friction points throughout the sales process by streamlining sales motions, automating administrative tasks, and enhancing data accessibility to remove obstacles that slow down the sales cycle, is vital for high performance. It includes assessing the effectiveness of CRM systems, automation tools, and digital platforms in facilitating smoother transitions between sales stages, improving lead qualification and follow-up processes, and enabling sales teams to focus more on selling and less on manual, time-consuming tasks. The goal is to understand how technology investments directly contribute to faster deal closures and more efficient sales workflows.

5. Sales Culture

Insights on Culture

In the fast-paced world of sales, a company's culture is the invisible force that shapes its success. Just as a computer's operating system determines its performance and capabilities, a sales organisation's culture sets the stage for its achievements. Building a vibrant and engaging sales culture that attracts and retains top talent is no small feat, particularly in an era where younger generations seek not only financial rewards but also a deep sense of purpose in their work. Developing a culture that motivates, inspires, and drives performance has become a critical priority for sales leaders.

At the core of this cultural transformation lies a relentless focus on excellence. Mediocrity and complacency have no place in a high-performance sales culture. Leaders must be unwavering in their commitment to setting and upholding high standards, even when it means making difficult decisions or having uncomfortable conversations.

Equally essential is the hands-on involvement and visibility of senior executives, particularly the CEO and CSO, in the sales organisation. By being present, engaged, and client-facing, these leaders demonstrate their dedication to the team's success and foster an environment of openness, responsibility, and teamwork.

When salespeople have confidence in their leaders and willingly follow their direction, it creates a positive and empowering atmosphere that ignites passion, motivation, and engagement. Clear performance metrics, shared openly and honestly, promote a culture of accountability and continuous improvement, while friendly competition encourages individuals to push themselves and each other to new heights of achievement.

One of the most significant obstacles to cultural transformation is when leaders fail to embody the change they seek to inspire. Leaders must lead by example, modelling the mindsets and behaviours they wish to see in their teams. They must communicate the link between the desired cultural attributes and business performance consistently and authentically from the outset. Additionally, change must be reinforced through incentives, with rewards, recognition, and opportunities for growth aligned with the behaviours that contribute to the organisation's success, especially collaboration across different functions.

Hallmarks of Sales Culture Excellence

1. **Zero Tolerance for Under Performance:** The absence of corrosive sentimentality and destructive ambiguity, plus the willingness to have the difficult conversations and make hard decisions is enormously clarifying.

2. **Active CEO and CSO Involvement:** The CEO and CSO are actively involved and visible in the sales organisation, fostering a culture of transparency, accountability, and collaboration. They are visible and accessible to the sales team, always client-facing, and have their eye on details and operations without being controlling.

3. **Leadership Endorsement:** When salespeople endorse and willingly follow their leaders, it creates a positive and empowering work environment that drives success, motivation, and engagement.

4. **High Levels of Trust:** A high-performance sales culture is built on a foundation of trust, which enables open communication, collaboration, and information sharing among team members.

5. **Cohesion, Teamwork and Collaboration:** A strong sense of unity and teamwork exists, with individuals working together towards common goals, fostering a culture of shared success.

6. **Personal Accountability:** Each team member takes personal responsibility for their targets and outcomes, fostering a culture of ownership, commitment, and continuous improvement.

7. **Transparent Performance Metrics:** Performance metrics and outcomes are openly shared, promoting an environment of honesty, accountability, and constructive feedback.

8. **Healthy Competition:** Healthy competition exists, encouraging individuals to strive for excellence without undermining others, fostering a culture of collaboration and shared success.

9. **Client-Centricity:** The needs and expectations of clients are at the heart of the sales process, guiding strategies and actions, and driving long-term client relationships and loyalty.

10. **Adaptability and Agility:** The culture embodies adaptability and agility, enabling the team to quickly respond to market changes, client needs, and technological advancements.

11. **Continuous Learning and Development:** Ongoing training and professional development opportunities are provided, ensuring that the sales team remains at the cutting edge of industry trends and sales methodologies.

12. **Effective Communication:** Clear and effective communication channels exist, facilitating the free flow of information and ideas within the team and with clients.

13. **Empowerment and Autonomy:** Sales professionals are given the autonomy to make decisions and take actions that align with the company's strategic goals, fostering a sense of empowerment and ownership.

14. **Recognition and Reward:** Achievements and contributions are recognised and rewarded, motivating individuals, reinforcing positive behaviours, and fostering a culture of continuous improvement.

15. **Feedback Culture:** Constructive feedback is regularly sought and given, contributing to personal growth, performance improvement, and a culture of continuous learning and development.

Assessing Sales Culture

In the intrinsic tapestry of organisational dynamics, the influence of leadership on sales culture stands out for its magnitude. Leaders, by virtue of their positions, cast long shadows over the sales culture, shaping it not only through deliberate actions but also through the subtleties of their demeanour and the unspoken messages they convey. Sales teams invariably align their priorities, care about what their leaders care about, and, most critically, emulate the behaviours exhibited by those at the helm. For example, leaders who exhibit traits of arrogance or a cavalier attitude, coupled with a lack of attention to detail, inadvertently sow these tendencies into the fabric of the sales culture. The result is an environment where operational rigour and process discipline are sidelined, giving way to a culture that values bravado over diligence. Similarly, a sales leader who operates in isolation, neglecting the cultivation of relationships with peers in other functions, fosters a sales culture that is insular and disconnected from the broader organisational ecosystem.

It would not be going too far to say that the characters and styles of sales leaders do more than just influence the sales culture; they become its very foundation. Critiques of the sales culture, whether explicit or implied, thus reflect directly upon the leadership, particularly the Head of Sales. Approach the discovery of culture and any negative feedback with the dials on emotional intelligence and political acumen turned high, or risk fracturing relationships.

1: Active CEO and CSO Involvement
How actively involved and visible are the CEO and CSO within the sales organisation to foster a culture of transparency, accountability, and collaboration?

Assessing their level of active involvement is crucial for understanding how leadership fosters the desired culture. Their visibility, accessibility, client-facing activities, and attention to details without being controlling indicate a leadership style that supports and energises the sales culture.

2: Leadership Endorsement

To what extent do salespeople endorse and willingly follow their leaders, creating a positive and empowering work environment?

Leadership endorsement from the sales team is a key indicator of a positive and empowering work environment. This question explores the dynamics between sales leaders and their teams, focusing on mutual respect, inspiration, and the leaders' ability to act as role models for the desired culture.

3: High Levels of Trust

How is a foundation of trust established within the sales team to enable open communication, collaboration, and information sharing?

Is there evidence of high trust or its antithesis? Trust remains a glue. Assessing if and how trust is cultivated and maintained within the team is critical for understanding the health and effectiveness of the sales culture.

4: Cohesion, Teamwork, and Collaboration

What mechanisms are in place to ensure a strong sense of unity and teamwork, with individuals working together towards common goals?

How does the trust, camaraderie, and friendship among leaders of different revenue functions impact the culture of the entire sales organisation?

The relationships among leaders of different revenue functions play a critical role in shaping the overall culture. The levels of trust, camaraderie, and mutual respect among these leaders influence the broader sales culture, foster a unified approach to achieving revenue goals, encourage cross-functional collaboration, and set a tone of solidarity and shared purpose that permeates the entire organisation.

5: Personal Accountability and Consequence Management

How does the sales culture promote personal accountability for targets and outcomes among team members?

What happens if targets are consistently not met?

Personal accountability is a cornerstone of a high-performance sales culture. Assessing the culture's emphasis on ownership, commitment, and continuous improvement is key to understanding its impact on performance. Sales organisations that tolerate missed targets and other indicators of poor performance guarantee their erosion.

6: Transparent Performance Metrics
Are performance metrics and outcomes openly shared within the team to promote an environment of honesty, accountability, and constructive feedback?

Transparency in performance metrics is essential for creating an environment where honesty, accountability, and constructive feedback thrive. In sales organisations that conceal poor performance from team scrutiny, performance dies.

7: Healthy Competition
How is healthy competition encouraged within the sales team to motivate excellence without undermining collaboration? Can one find evidence of mechanisms that promote healthy competition?

Healthy competition within the sales team drives individuals to strive for excellence. Leaderboards and awards are key. Assessing how competition is balanced with collaboration is crucial for ensuring that it contributes positively to the culture.

8: Client-Centricity
In what ways is client-centricity embedded in the sales process and culture, guiding strategies and driving long-term relationships and loyalty?

Client-centricity and a healthy obsession with customer experience should be at the heart of the sales culture. This question assesses how the sales team prioritises client needs and expectations, and how this focus drives strategic execution.

9: Adaptability and Agility

How does the culture embody adaptability and agility, enabling quick responses to market changes, client needs, and technological changes? How responsive and quick to act is the sales organisation, or is it encumbered by bureaucracy?

The ability of the sales team to adapt and respond quickly to external changes is a key aspect of a dynamic sales culture. Agility is so important, and bureaucratic bumbling is a killer of great cultures.

10: Effective Communication

How are clear and effective communication channels maintained within the team, facilitating the free flow of information and ideas? How well do collaborators in the sales engine communicate, strategise, and solve problems?

Signs and signals of poor communication are troubling. Great communication is the lifeblood of any group striving to achieve anything significant and perform optimally. Open and honest communication without fear of reprisals, regular feedback, transparency, information sharing, and sufficient positive forums are all important hallmarks.

6. Sales Leadership

Insights on Sales Leadership

The pivotal role of sales within the global operational framework was profoundly articulated by a Chief Executive I once consulted for, who delineated the organisation into two distinct groups: those in sales and everyone else. This delineation reshaped my perception of the sales function and underscored its paramount importance and inherent complexity. Sales engines, as intricate sub-systems, necessitate a symbiotic network of collaborations to flourish. Their health and efficacy are critical, yet challenging to optimise, given their reliance on multifaceted interactions. This discourse aims to dissect the evaluation process of a sales engine's vitality, employing a systematic approach against global benchmarks. We shall navigate through the foundational elements, traverse the sales funnel from inception to closure, and explore strategies for stabilisation and expansion.

The assessment of leadership within the sales domain emerges as a formidable challenge, primarily due to the nebulous nature of leadership and culture, coupled with the intricacies of quantification and measurement. The quest for causality amidst a labyrinth of influencing factors often leads to correlations that, while insightful, rest on precarious grounds. How, then, can anyone discern the robustness and vigour of sales leadership? Is it feasible to equate leadership efficacy with tangible sales metrics? My experience has shown that sales teams can exhibit stellar performance over consecutive quarters, only to succumb to an unsustainable culture. Thus, a framework for evaluation is indispensable, one that elucidates critical inquiries.

The complexity and sophistication required in leading B2B selling organisations have expanded significantly, raising the competency bar for sales leadership. Achieving consistent execution, operational rigour, and process discipline is paramount, yet challenging. Modern leaders must co-create a compelling vision, drive engagement, and master cross-functional influence due to the interconnectedness of sales with other departments. Sales leadership is crucial for setting priorities and modelling behaviours that establish the cultural foundation of an organisation, driving exceptional performance. Leaders must navigate the intricacies of the corporate institutions, ensuring their teams are agile, aligned with customer needs, and prepared for market dynamics. Members of the sales engine will generally obsess over what their leaders obsess about, value and prioritise what they value, track what they track, and discard what they discard. They cast a big shadow over the sales organisation. The best I've worked with possess a unique set of skills, experiences, and attributes that enable them to inspire, motivate, and guide their teams to success.

Hallmarks of Sales Leadership Excellence

1. **Personal Accomplishment:** Sales leaders consistently achieve their targets, lead by example, and inspire their teams through their own actions and results. They set the bar high and demonstrate what is possible through their own personal success.

2. **Strategic and Tactical Acumen:** Effective sales leaders possess the ability to translate high-level strategies into actionable sales roadmaps. They anticipate potential obstacles, adapt tactics when necessary, and ensure that their teams are always aligned with the overall strategic vision.

3. **Experience and Expertise:** Exceptional sales leaders bring a wealth of industry knowledge and people management experience to the table. They leverage their expertise to guide their teams, make informed decisions, and navigate complex sales situations with confidence.

4. **Planning and Execution:** Sales leaders excel at comprehensive planning, ensuring that strategy execution is well-coordinated across short-term, medium-term, and long-term timeframes. They break down goals into manageable steps and ensure that their teams have the resources and support needed to execute effectively.

5. **Client-Centricity:** Top sales leaders prioritise client needs and value-drivers, fostering a culture of customer-centricity within

their teams. They focus on building long-term client relationships, understanding that sustainable success comes from creating value for customers.

6. **Continuous Learning:** The best sales leaders are lifelong learners, constantly staying abreast of industry trends, best practices, and emerging technologies. They encourage their teams to embrace a growth mindset and provide opportunities for continuous learning and development.

7. **Gutsy and Innovative:** Exceptional sales leaders are not afraid to take calculated risks on well-thought-out ideas. They foster a culture of creativity and innovation, encouraging their teams to think outside the box and explore new approaches to sales challenges.

8. **Administration and Organisation:** While sales leaders are often associated with big-picture thinking, the best ones also pay close attention to detail. They ensure that administrative tasks are completed promptly, that no backlog accumulates, and that their teams are well-organised and efficient.

9. **Meeting Facilitation:** Sales leaders are skilled facilitators, able to conduct meetings that are engaging, participatory, and results oriented. They ensure that meetings have clear objectives, that all voices are heard, and that decisions are made collaboratively.

10. **Inspiration and Motivation:** Great sales leaders have the ability to make the strategic journey exciting, relevant, and inspiring for their teams. They communicate the vision in a way that resonates with each individual, fostering a sense of purpose and motivation.

11. **Problem-Solving:** When challenges arise, top sales leaders are able to analyse the situation, gather relevant information, and take decisive action. They are effective problem-solvers, able to navigate complex issues and find solutions that benefit both the client and the organisation.

12. **Communication and Influence:** Exceptional sales leaders are master communicators, able to articulate ideas clearly, listen attentively, and influence others regardless of their title or position. They build strong relationships based on trust and respect, and are able to rally their teams around a common goal.

13. **Support and Protection:** The best sales leaders are fierce advocates for their teams, always promoting and protecting the interests of their people. They provide the support and resources needed for success, and stand up for their teams in the face of challenges or adversity.

14. **Empowerment and Ownership:** Sales leaders foster a culture of empowerment and ownership, encouraging their teams to take initiative, make decisions, and participate actively in the sales process. They provide guidance and support but trust their teams to take ownership of their work.

15. **Growth and Development:** Exceptional sales leaders are committed to the growth and development of their teams. They provide opportunities for learning, mentor their team members, and actively work to build a pipeline of future leaders who will drive the organisation forward.

16. **Collaboration with Other Functional Heads:** Top sales leaders understand the importance of collaboration and alignment across the organisation. They work closely with other functional heads to ensure that sales strategies are in sync with overall business objectives, and that all departments are working together towards common goals.

17. **Data-Driven Leadership:** The best sales leaders make decisions based on data and insights, not just intuition. They leverage market research, customer analytics, and sales data to inform their strategies and tactics, and are able to anticipate trends and shifts in the market.

18. **Cohesion within the Sales Engine:** Sales leaders foster a strong sense of camaraderie and cohesion within their teams.

They create a shared sense of identity, often with a unique lexicon and set of rituals, and encourage healthy competition that drives everyone to perform at their best.

19. **Experienced and Skilful Leadership:** Exceptional sales leaders bring a wealth of experience to the role, with a proven track record of success and a robust network of mentors and advisors. They are able to draw on this experience to navigate challenges, seize opportunities, and guide their teams to success.

20. **Frontline Engagement by Leadership:** The best sales leaders are not afraid to get their hands dirty and engage directly with customers. They have their own personal KPIs and sales targets, and lead by example in pursuing new business and strengthening client relationships.

21. **Endorsement by the Sales Team:** Great sales leaders earn the respect, admiration, and endorsement of their teams through their actions, their integrity, and their commitment to collective success. They are viewed not just as bosses, but as mentors, coaches, and allies in the pursuit of sales excellence.

22. **A Culture of Performance and Celebration:** Exceptional sales leaders create a culture where performance is expected, recognised, and celebrated. They conduct regular coaching sessions to help team members improve and make a point of publicly celebrating individual and team successes, fostering a sense of pride and accomplishment within the sales organisation.

Assessing Sales Leadership Excellence

Navigating the terrain of sales leadership weaknesses and areas for development within the broader context of sales turnaround is a task fraught with complexity and nuance. At the heart of this lies the dual imperative of delivering candid feedback to improve leadership performance while simultaneously fostering a positive relationship with the sales leader, a central figure in the transformation process. The assessment/correction/improvement process is not easy and will require great skill and sensitivity. It should also involve observing the leader in action, as nothing provides more layers of context and nuance as dynamics unfold, and feedback will land better with this in place.

1: Personal Accomplishment
When examining the biographies and achievements of the sales leadership, does one find a consistent track record of personal accomplishment?

Leaders with a track record of achieving personal targets in previous and their current role set a benchmark for excellence within the team, establishing credibility and fostering a culture of high performance. Absence of this can lead to diminished respect and trust, undermining leadership effectiveness.

2: Strategic and Tactical Acumen
How, if at all, do sales leaders translate organisational strategy into actionable sales plans?

The ability to craft and execute detailed sales plans based on strategic objectives is crucial for guiding the team towards achieving business goals. Sales organisations need to feel like their efforts contribute towards a strategic mission. Lack of strategic acumen, or just plain neglect of this, can result in people feeling dislocated and misaligned.

3: Experience and Expertise
What level of industry knowledge and people management expertise do sales managers possess? Are sales leaders able to leverage their experience and networks to guide and mentor the team?

Deep industry knowledge and effective people management are foundational for informed decision-making and strategic guidance. Without these, leaders may struggle to navigate challenges or inspire confidence among team members. Experienced leaders provide valuable insights and guidance, leverage their networks, and naturally enhance team capabilities.

4: Planning and Execution
With what degree of structure and consistency do sales managers execute the sales strategy?

Disciplined, structured, focused execution ensures the right behaviours are carried out at the right time, consistently. Resources are optimally allocated, accountability is high, and results flow from there. Haphazard execution of the mission is ineffective.

5: Client-Centricity and Engagement
In what ways, if at all, do sales leaders personally prioritise building long-term, mutually beneficial relationships with clients?

How involved are sales leaders in direct customer engagement and achieving personal KPIs?

Sales managers need to be on the front line engaging with clients, building relationships. This is not to be confused with meddling in deals but rather a client-centricity that aligns sales efforts with customer needs, driving loyalty and team success. Direct involvement in sales activities keeps leaders grounded and informed, enhancing team morale and performance. Detachment from frontline activities can lead to disconnection from the team's realities and challenges.

6: Administration and Organisation
How do sales leaders manage day-to-day operations to prevent administrative backlog?

Efficient administration ensures smooth operations and allows the team to focus on selling and remain undistracted by all kinds of outstanding issues and lingering nuances. Poor administrative management can lead to inefficiencies and frustration.

7: Meeting Facilitation
How effectively do sales leaders structure and facilitate meetings to ensure productive use of time and resources, and the quick resolution of problems?

What indicators demonstrate cohesion and a positive competitive culture within the sales team?

Productive meetings that are positive, well-structured, participative, and crisp in execution enhance team morale, alignment, and decision-making. Problems get raised and solved quickly in these forums. Ineffective meetings waste time, dilute focus, and leave problems unresolved. Cohesion and healthy competition, evident in meetings, drive team performance and morale.

8: Support and Protection
How do sales leaders support and protect their team from external interference? How do they address conflict situations with sales collaborators?

Protecting the team from politics, noise, and any negative influence from senior leaders in other functions fosters a safe and focused working environment, but also loyalty and allegiance. Managers who push conflict situations under the carpet, instead of confronting them head-on with the aim to bring about resolution, guarantee those issues will fester and hurt the team's productivity. Failure to lead with a protective style will expose the team to unnecessary distractions and leave them feeling ungrounded.

9: Collaboration with Other Functional Heads
How effectively do sales managers collaborate with heads of other functions to align the revenue engine with organisational goals?

Cross-functional collaboration ensures strategic alignment and operational efficiency. Siloed operations can lead to misaligned objectives and inefficiencies. When managers collaborate, it sets a tone and shapes the culture dramatically, for the positive.

10: Data-Driven Leadership and Performance Coaching
Is the strategic planning and execution, as well as the performance management and coaching, underpinned by data-driven insights?

Data-driven decision-making enhances strategic foresight and operational effectiveness. Reliance on intuition alone can lead to misguided strategies and low confidence in the plan. Performance coaching conversations, executed on a set cadence and informed by performance data, are essential for high performance.

7. Capability

In the realm of B2B sales, the success of an organisation is intrinsically linked to its sales capabilities, which are built upon the foundation of specific competencies. Sales capabilities represent an organisation's capacity to effectively utilise resources to achieve its sales goals. These capabilities are a symbiotic blend of broad organisational abilities and specific individual competencies. Competencies, the building blocks of capabilities, are the skills and processes tailored to specific tasks within the sales process. They enable sales professionals to navigate the complexities of the B2B landscape, foster growth, and maintain a competitive edge.

Developing top-tier sales capabilities requires a holistic approach that integrates comprehensive competency assessments, exceptional training, and a culture of continuous feedback. The journey begins with training but is solidified through real-world application, where sales professionals apply their acquired knowledge in practical settings. Sales leaders play a crucial role in this transition by providing guidance, feedback, and support, refining strategies, and enhancing performance.

The Capability Workstream is a critical component in sales turnarounds, focusing on developing the necessary skills and competencies to navigate new strategic landscapes. It identifies skill gaps, builds essential systems, and translates turnaround objectives into actionable learning curriculums. Through targeted training and coaching, this workstream ensures that changes are effectively implemented and embraced, driving organisational success in a competitive sales environment.

10 Hallmarks of Sales Capability Excellence

1. **Coaching Alignment:** Sales leaders align coaching interventions with sales productivity and performance goals, ensuring targeted development and maximised impact.

2. **Personalised Learning:** Organisations leverage technology to create personalised learning pathways for strategic skill acquisition, focusing on the most critical areas for performance improvement.

3. **Diverse Learning Modalities**: Sales teams adopt diverse learning modalities to enhance engagement and knowledge retention, catering to different learning preferences.

4. **Performance Integration:** Capability development is integrated into structured goal setting and performance evaluation processes, linking competency growth directly to sales performance.

5. **Continuous Learning Culture:** Organisations foster a culture of continuous learning within the sales team, with adequate investments in high-quality training.

6. **Practical Application and Feedback:** Sales leaders facilitate the practical application of learned competencies and provide feedback for continuous improvement, transforming theoretical knowledge into tangible capabilities.

7. **Leadership Involvement:** Sales leaders and team managers actively guide, coach, and support the development of sales capabilities, influencing the practical application of skills in the field.

8. **Data-Driven Development:** Organisations utilise data from sales interactions, customer feedback, and performance metrics to inform capability development, ensuring training efforts are focused on areas with the greatest potential impact.

9. **Comprehensive Assessments:** Sales teams conduct comprehensive competency assessments to identify areas for development and strengths, guiding effective capability development.

10. **Sales Assessment Centre (SAC):** Organisations implement a well-designed SAC to provide a holistic, objective, and developmental approach to evaluating sales personnel, enabling informed decisions regarding talent development, role placement, and succession planning.

Assessing Capability Development Effectiveness

When assessing a company's Sales Capability Building System, tread carefully, recognising the intricate dynamics between sales leadership and HR. Sensitivity and respect are needed. Understand that capability development is often a collaborative effort between sales and HR. Critiquing these systems can inadvertently be seen as critiquing both departments. Given that sales leaders typically do not hold direct accountability over capability development, their engagement requires a nuanced understanding of roles and responsibilities, often encapsulated by the RACI framework.

Recognise HR's invaluable expertise in identifying skill gaps, developing competencies, and fostering continuous learning environments. Their role is foundational. Attempting to diagnose, improve, or modify these systems without HR's input and cooperation can lead to misunderstandings, resistance, and potentially, conflict. Engage in constructive dialogue with HR from the outset. Share insights and objectives transparently, emphasising shared goals. My objective is best achieved through a partnership that leverages the strengths and expertise of both sales leadership and HR.

1: Performance Coaching Culture and Alignment
Is there evidence of a coaching culture marked by consistency and focus? How are coaching interventions aligned with improving sales productivity and performance?

Aligning coaching with sales goals, and a system like OKRs, ensures targeted development and maximises the impact on performance. Absence of this alignment can lead to unfocused development efforts and missed performance enhancement opportunities.

2: Personalised Learning Pathways
How is technology leveraged to create personalised learning pathways for strategic skill acquisition?

Personalised learning pathways focus development on skills with the highest impact on sales performance, ensuring efficient and effective capability building. Without strategic personalisation and effective use of technology, training may not address the most critical areas for performance improvement.

3: Multi-Modal Content Delivery
In what ways does the organisation adopt diverse learning modalities to enhance engagement and retention?

Antiquated learning and classroom-only training will be met with cynicism. Diverse learning modalities cater to different learning preferences, increasing engagement and knowledge retention. A lack of variety in content delivery can hinder learning effectiveness and engagement.

4: Integration with Performance Metrics
How is capability development integrated into structured goal setting and performance evaluation processes?

Formal integration of capability development with performance metrics ensures that competency growth is directly linked to sales performance, making development efforts more relevant and measurable. Without this integration, development activities may not be effectively focused on improving sales outcomes.

5: Continuous Learning Culture
What mechanisms are in place to foster a culture of continuous learning within the sales organisation?

How adequate are investments in training and how good is that training?

A culture that prioritises continuous learning ensures that the sales team remains adaptable and competitive. The absence of a learning culture and investments in quality training can lead to stagnation and a decline in competitive positioning.

6: Real-World Application and Feedback Loop
How does the organisation facilitate the practical application of learned competencies and provide feedback for continuous improvement?

The transition from theoretical learning to practical application, supported by a robust feedback loop, is critical for transforming competencies into tangible capabilities. Most of what is learned in the classroom is forgotten. Lack of practical application and feedback can hinder the effective development of capabilities.

7: Leadership Role in Capability Development
What role do sales leaders and team managers play in guiding, coaching, and supporting the development of sales capabilities?

Sales leaders and team managers are crucial in providing the guidance and support needed for effective capability development, influencing the practical application of skills in the field. When managers are detached from development it significantly impedes development efforts and undermines investments in training.

8: Data-Driven Skill Development
How does the organisation use data from sales interactions, customer feedback, and performance metrics to inform capability development and make it really personalised?

Leveraging data to inform skill development ensures that training efforts are focused on areas with the greatest potential impact on sales productivity. Ignoring data can lead to stale and generic development experiences that fall flat.

9: Strategic Competency Assessments
How comprehensive are the organisation's competency assessments in identifying areas for development and strengths?

Comprehensive competency assessments are foundational for identifying strategic areas for development and leveraging strengths, guiding effective capability development. Inadequate assessments can lead to a lack of focus in development efforts, missing critical areas for improvement.

Insights on Sales Competencies

The delineation of core competencies intrinsic to the performance of any B2B sales organisation is pivotal for understanding the underpinnings of successful sales strategies and operations. These competencies enable a sales organisation to effectively navigate the complexities of the B2B landscape, fostering sustainable growth and competitive advantage.

Here are 18 Core Competencies that I personally prize most. They are not merely a collection of skills but complex amalgamations that enable the execution of high-level tasks and actions, foundational and critical.

1. **Market Analysis and Segmentation:** Mastery in analysing market trends, identifying lucrative customer segments, and understanding the competitive landscape to discern the most promising opportunities for the organisation's offerings.

2. **Value Proposition Development:** The art of crafting compelling value propositions that resonate deeply with target customer segments, based on a profound understanding of their needs and how the organisation's solutions uniquely address those needs.

3. **Strategic Planning and Alignment:** The capacity for developing, articulating, and executing sales strategies in harmony with broader organisational goals, encompassing setting clear objectives, defining KPIs, and ensuring sales efforts are congruent with the overall business strategy.

4. **Prospecting and Lead Generation:** The foundational competency of identifying and engaging potential customers proactively, essential for building a robust sales pipeline through both outbound and inbound lead generation strategies.

5. **Sales Process Management:** The ability to design, implement, and oversee a structured sales process that guides sales activities from prospecting to closing, understanding sales cycle stages, managing sales activities, and employing sales methodologies effectively.

6. **Forecasting and Pipeline Management:** Competence in predicting sales revenue and managing the sales pipeline to

ensure a consistent flow of business, through analysing sales data, identifying trends, and making informed predictions about future sales performance.

7. **Negotiation and Closing:** The skill to negotiate effectively with prospects and close deals, requiring a deep understanding of the customer's business, the ability to articulate value, and the skill to navigate objections to reach mutually beneficial agreements.

8. **Customer Relationship Management:** The ability to forge and sustain strong relationships with customers from initial contact through to post-sale and renewal, understanding customer needs, providing ongoing support, and fostering loyalty.

9. **Stakeholder Engagement:** The capacity to engage and influence various stakeholders within the customer's organisation, crucial for navigating complex B2B sales environments, including decision-makers and influencers.

10. **Collaboration and Teamwork:** The ability to work effectively within the sales team and across departments to achieve sales objectives, sharing best practices, learning from successes and failures, and supporting team members.

11. **Strategic Partnership Development:** Identifying and cultivating strategic partnerships to extend market reach and enhance the organisation's ability to meet customer needs more comprehensively.

12. **Lead Generation and Qualification:** The process of generating leads and effectively qualifying them, ensuring that sales efforts are focused on prospects with the highest potential for conversion.

13. **Pipeline Management:** The strategic oversight of the sales pipeline, ensuring a balanced and strategic approach to moving prospects through to closing.

14. **Contract Negotiation:** The ability to negotiate contracts that meet both the organisation's and the customer's needs, ensuring legal compliance and mutual satisfaction.

15. **Value Creation for Customers:** The continuous effort to create and demonstrate value for customers, enhancing customer satisfaction and loyalty.

16. **Business Case Development:** Developing compelling business cases that clearly articulate the value and benefits of the organisation's solutions to customers.

17. **Economic Value and ROI Estimation:** Estimating and articulating the economic value and potential ROI of solutions to customers, supporting the customer's decision-making process.

18. **Storytelling for Sales Impact:** The proficiency in capturing salient details, crafting a compelling narrative by weaving the organisation's offerings, value propositions, and differentiators so it resonates on a personal level with the target audience and delivering it in such a manner that it catalyses action.

Assessing Sales Competencies

The most effective way to assess these competencies inside a sales organisation is through a well-designed and executed Sales Assessment Centre (SAC). Some might argue that one should simply analyse sales results to determine competencies, but this is not accurate. While analysing sales results is important for evaluating sales performance, it should not be considered the sole indicator of sales competencies. Relying exclusively on sales results has several limitations, such as a short-term focus, lack of context, lack of developmental insights, ignoring team dynamics, and limited predictive value. In contrast, a comprehensive SAC provides a more holistic, objective, and developmental approach to evaluating sales personnel. By combining simulations, SME scoring, live feedback, panel interviews, and competency-based assessments, an SAC offers a more reliable and actionable assessment of an individual's competencies, enabling organisations to make informed decisions regarding talent development, role placement, and succession planning, ultimately driving long-term sales success.

8. Talent Management

Insights on Talent Management

Building a high-performing sales talent engine is one of the most difficult yet vital capabilities for companies relying on sales for growth and profitability. Most fail due to the complexity and penalties of failure. Sales talent strategy encompasses five interlocked phases:

1. Defining and sourcing the right talent

2. Selecting and hiring top performers

3. Motivating people and rewarding achievement

4. Developing skills and capability

5. Retaining the best by creating an elite environment

Weaknesses in any part compromise the whole. Most sales organisations struggle with retention and continuity, with high costs of replacing lost sales capacity. Most compensation plans are criticised. Key factors for this coveted yet elusive success include poor candidate sourcing, flawed selection processes, unclear performance attributes, and cursory onboarding. Proof lies in high turnover, missed quotas, and non-strategic replacement hiring. Building a sales talent surplus requires excelling across the integrated spectrum of talent strategy and flaws almost always predict wider issues in sales execution.

Hallmarks of Talent Management Excellence

1. **Strategic Talent Acquisition:** Organisations prioritise character, work ethic, motivational drive, and resilience when recruiting sales talent. They understand that these fundamental qualities are essential for success in the demanding and competitive world of sales.

2. **Efficient and Engaging Recruitment Process:** Sales organisations continuously refine their recruitment processes to ensure efficiency and a positive candidate experience.

They implement net recommender scores and actively seek candidate feedback to identify areas for improvement.

3. **Rigorous and Fulfilling Onboarding:** Onboarding programmes are designed to be rigorous, ensuring that new hires are well-prepared for their roles. At the same time, these programmes prioritise personal fulfilment, helping new team members feel valued, connected, and motivated. The success of onboarding is measured through time to productivity, ensuring that new hires are quickly integrated and contributing to the organisation's goals.

4. **Accreditation and Empowerment:** Sales organisations invest in comprehensive accreditation programmes that ensure sales personnel are fully prepared and confident in their abilities. These programmes set high standards for knowledge, skills, and performance, empowering sales professionals to excel in their roles.

5. **Compelling Retention Strategies:** Organisations develop meaningful benefits and tailored remuneration plans to retain top sales talent. They offer uncapped commissions, recognising and rewarding high performance. These strategies go beyond financial incentives and include opportunities for professional development, work-life balance initiatives, and a supportive and inclusive work environment.

6. **Superior Sales Enablement:** Sales teams are equipped with top-tier technology, content, tools, and information to excel in their roles. Organisations invest in state-of-the-art CRM systems, sales automation tools, and robust content libraries. They ensure that sales professionals have access to the latest market insights, competitive intelligence, and best practices.

7. **Excellence in Sales Management:** Sales managers provide supportive coaching, offering constructive feedback and guidance to help their team members grow and succeed. They celebrate successes, recognising and appreciating the efforts and achievements of their team.

8. **Performance-Based Culture:** Organisations foster a performance-based culture that recognises and rewards achievements. They set clear performance metrics and celebrate those who exceed expectations. While the environment is competitive, it remains supportive and collaborative.

9. **Flexible Career Pathway and Innovative Environments:** Sales organisations demonstrate a strong commitment to the professional growth and development of their team members. They offer flexible career pathways, allowing sales professionals to explore different roles and opportunities within the organisation.

Assessing Talent Management

Prioritising talent management initiatives should be informed by evaluating sales team's capabilities, effectiveness of current strategies, and specific challenges and opportunities. Necessity and scope vary across contexts. Considerable financial losses can accrue due to low tenure, long ramp-up times, and expensive turmoil and attrition.

Key Questions for Assessment:

1. *Does the company have a high-performing, cross-functional talent operation?*

   A successful talent strategy consistently produces quality fit for purpose. Look for solid evidence of a strong talent pipeline and retention of top performers.

2. *Is the talent pipeline strong?*

   A robust pipeline, built over many quarters with candidates at various stages, is essential for mitigating vulnerability and supporting growth and profitability.

3. *Does the company have a defined talent profile for recruiting and growing young guns into superstars?*

Focusing on recruiting high potential individuals and nurturing them into top performers can be more sustainable than frequently seeking experienced salespeople.

4. *Is the end-to-end process fine-tuned for candidate satisfaction?*

The recruitment process must be efficient, organised, and respectful of candidates' time and aspirations. Fast, streamlined processes signal respect and give a competitive edge.

5. *Does onboarding qualify as rigorous, personally fulfilling, and effective?*

Effective onboarding is crucial for new hires to reach performance targets promptly. The process should be thorough, challenging, and engaging, with clear metrics for success.

6. *Is the right to sell earned through an 'accreditation to sell' process?*

An in-depth, challenging accreditation process ensures sales personnel are knowledgeable, competent, and confident, setting a high standard for sales excellence.

7. *Does the company pay well and make it hard for superstars to leave?*

Competitive compensation, meaningful benefits, and a fair, uncapped commission structure are essential for retaining top talent. Strategies should avoid demotivating practices and focus on tailored remuneration and non-monetary incentives.

8. *Is sales enablement above reproach and criticism?*

Top performers expect and deserve the best sales enablement tools and resources. Companies must ensure their sales teams have access to the latest and most effective tools, content, and technology.

9. *Is sales management up to task, with teams endorsing and following their lead?*

Effective sales management is crucial for retention. Respect and endorsement from sales teams indicate supportive coaching and a culture that celebrates success and fosters loyalty and high performance.

10. *How mature are the company's talent management practices, aligning talent development with strategic business goals?*

Mature talent management involves strategic alignment between talent development and business objectives, ensuring talent growth directly contributes to the company's strategic goals. This includes commitment to continuous learning, career development opportunities, and clear pathways for progression. It also entails leveraging data and analytics to inform talent decisions. Look for evidence of structured talent review processes, succession planning, and investment in leadership development as indicators of maturity.

9. Performance Management Systems

Insights on Performance Management

Excellence in Sales Performance Management Systems (SPMS) is marked by a blend of strategic alignment, technological innovation, and a culture that champions continuous improvement and growth. These systems stand out for their comprehensive approach to driving and sustaining high sales performance across organisations.

Forward-thinking clients have transformed the traditional annual performance review into a dynamic, ongoing dialogue. Feedback, goal discussions, and development planning are now continuous, allowing for immediate adjustments and more prompt recognition of achievements and areas needing improvement. Regular, informal check-ins have replaced the once-a-year review, fostering a culture of development and forward-looking improvement. The use of 360-degree feedback and advanced software supports this continuous approach, making feedback and goal management more efficient and tailored. The emphasis on both individual and team performance underscores the critical role of collaboration and collective success in meeting business goals.

Hallmarks of Sales Performance Management Excellence

1. **Strategic Alignment:** A robust SPMS ensures that sales objectives and targets are carefully aligned with the broader organisational goals and strategies. This alignment is crucial for ensuring that the sales team's efforts contribute directly to the overall success and growth of the company.

2. **Balanced Metrics:** An effective SPMS utilises a balanced combination of both quantitative and qualitative metrics to provide a holistic view of sales performance. While quantitative metrics such as sales volume, revenue, and market share are essential, qualitative metrics such as customer satisfaction, product knowledge, and teamwork are equally important.

3. **Continuous Feedback:** A modern SPMS shifts away from traditional, annual performance reviews and instead employs dynamic, continuous feedback mechanisms. This approach allows for real-time adjustments and improvements in sales performance.

4. **Frequent Check-ins:** In line with the emphasis on continuous feedback, an effective SPMS replaces annual reviews with regular, informal conversations focused on development and growth. These frequent check-ins provide opportunities for managers and sales team members to discuss progress, challenges, and opportunities in a more relaxed and collaborative setting.

5. **360-Degree Feedback:** A comprehensive SPMS employs feedback from multiple sources, including managers, peers, and direct reports. This 360-degree approach provides a more well-rounded view of an individual's performance and helps to identify strengths and areas for improvement that may not be apparent from a single perspective.

6. **Advanced Technology:** To facilitate continuous performance management and data-driven decision-making, a cutting-edge SPMS leverages advanced software and platforms. These technologies automate data collection, analysis, and reporting, allowing managers and sales team members to access real-time insights and track progress against goals.

7. **Team Performance Emphasis:** A forward-thinking SPMS recognises the importance of teamwork and collective outcomes in driving sales success. While individual performance is still important, the system places a strong emphasis on team-based metrics and incentives.

8. **Real-time Data and Customisation:** An advanced SPMS harnesses the power of real-time data and analytics to provide up-to-the-minute insights into sales performance. This data-driven approach allows managers to identify trends, spot opportunities, and make informed decisions based on the most current information available.

9. **Performance-Based Incentives:** A well-designed SPMS features structured incentive plans that are closely tied to performance metrics. These incentives may include bonuses, commissions, and other rewards that are directly linked to the achievement of specific sales goals and targets.

10. **Cultural Alignment and Actionable Insights:** Finally, an effective SPMS must be aligned with the organisation's overall culture and values. The system should reinforce the company's mission, vision, and guiding principles, and ensure that sales performance is measured and rewarded in a way that is consistent with these core tenets.

Assessing sales performance management

When assessing and changing performance management systems, tread with caution. Performance management is fraught with personal stakes, tied to individual aspirations, ego, and the need for recognition. The process intersects with personal identity and self-worth, making it potentially explosive. It is also linked to career advancement, status, and financial well-being, creating a complex web of dynamics where feedback can be perceived as commentary on one's value and future prospects.

Key Questions for Assessment:

1: Performance Metrics Alignment
How are personal metrics aligned with strategic goals, and what process updates them as objectives evolve?

This question assesses the alignment of performance metrics with broader organisational goals, highlighting the principle that effective performance management systems must be dynamic and adaptable to changing business strategies.

2: Realtime Feedback Mechanisms
What mechanisms provide real-time feedback, and how has this influenced the immediacy and relevance of coaching?

The focus here is on the systems that enable immediate feedback, emphasising the value of timely and specific feedback in facilitating rapid performance improvements and adjustments.

3: Performance Improvement Plans (PIPs)
How are PIPs structured, and what role do they play in addressing underperformance?

This question delves into the structure and effectiveness of PIPs, underscoring their importance in a comprehensive performance management strategy that seeks to uplift rather than penalise struggling sales personnel.

4: Coaching and Development Integration
How is coaching integrated into the regular performance management cycle, and what impact has this had on development?

It explores the integration of coaching into performance management, highlighting the principle that ongoing development and coaching are key to enhancing sales competencies and achieving long-term success.

5: Data-driven Decision Making
How does the PMS support data-driven decision making in sales strategies and operations?

The emphasis is on the role of data and analytics in informing sales strategies, highlighting the shift towards evidence-based decision making in sales management.

6: Impact on Sales Culture
How has the PMS influenced the sales culture, particularly collaboration, competition, and innovation?

It explores the broader cultural impact of the PMS, focusing on how the system has influenced the dynamics of collaboration, healthy competition, and innovation within the sales team.

7: Performance Appraisal

How do appraisal processes facilitate individual development and contribute to organisational goals? Is it accepted and endorsed, or criticised and resisted?

This question aims to uncover not just the procedural aspect of performance appraisals but also their strategic and developmental impact. The endorsement and effectiveness of the appraisal system in fostering growth and aligning individual performance with broader organisational objectives are crucial.

8: Quantification and Measurability

Can you describe the process for setting measurable outcomes or key results for individual and team objectives?

Adopt a structured approach to defining specific, measurable, achievable, relevant, and timebound key results, ensuring they are visible to all. This facilitates precise tracking of progress and achievement, enabling more accurate performance assessments.

9: Integration of Goals into Performance Management

How frequently are goal progress and achievements reviewed, and how is this integrated into the performance management cycle?

Regularly scheduled reviews of objectives and quantified results integrated into the performance management cycle allow for high levels of accountability and real-time adjustments and feedback.

10: Below-par Performance

How is below-par performance identified and addressed? How is it initially flagged, and what corrective actions or employment termination measures are taken?

Consistent below-par performance warrants ultimate punitive measures but also supportive and developmental approaches that should be integrated into the performance management system. What is desirable is a balance between maintaining high performance standards and fostering a culture of growth and improvement, providing sales personnel the opportunity to rebound from performance setbacks.

10. Sales Compensation

Insights on Sales Compensation

Sales compensation is a critical component of any successful sales strategy, as it directly influences the motivation, behaviour, and performance of the sales team. When a company fails to design and implement an effective sales compensation plan, the consequences can be far-reaching and detrimental to the organisation's overall success.

One of the most significant consequences of getting sales compensation wrong is the negative impact on motivation. If the compensation plan is poorly designed, with unclear targets, unrealistic goals, or inadequate rewards, sales team members may become discouraged and disengaged. This lack of motivation can lead to reduced effort, lower productivity, and ultimately, a decline in sales performance.

In addition to the impact on individual motivation, ineffective sales compensation can also hinder collaboration, particularly in global organisations. When compensation plans are not aligned across different regions, countries, or business units, it can create a sense of inequity and resentment among sales team members. This can lead to a breakdown in communication, knowledge sharing, and teamwork, as individuals become more focused on their own performance and less willing to support their colleagues.

Another critical consequence of getting sales compensation wrong is the inability to drive and motivate the right behaviours. If the sales compensation plan is not designed to support strategic shifts, sales team members may continue to focus on the wrong activities or metrics. This misalignment between compensation and strategic objectives can severely limit the organisation's ability to execute its desired sales transformation.

Furthermore, poorly designed sales compensation plans can lead to unintended consequences, such as encouraging unethical behaviour or short-term thinking. If the compensation plan places too much emphasis on individual performance, without adequate safeguards or balancing metrics, sales professionals may be tempted to engage in questionable practices, such as overpromising to customers, manipulating data, or neglecting important non-sales activities. Similarly, if the plan does not provide sufficient incentives for long-term success, such as customer retention or account development, sales team members may focus solely on closing deals in the short term, at the expense of building lasting customer relationships.

Hallmarks of excellence in Sales Compensation Design and Management

1. **Performance-Based Models:** Integrating base salary with variable components linked to individual, team, and organisational performance, ensuring sales efforts directly contribute to strategic goals and a high-performance culture.

2. **Tiered Commission Structures:** Offering increasing commission rates for exceeding sales targets, incentivising sales personnel to surpass expectations and significantly boost their earnings.

3. **Equity-Based Incentives:** Incorporating stock options or restricted stock units (RSUs) to align the sales team's interests with the company's long-term success, fostering ownership and commitment.

4. **Non-Monetary Recognition:** Implementing recognition programmes like awards, public acknowledgment, career development opportunities, and exclusive clubs for high achievers, recognising hard work and boosting job satisfaction and loyalty.

5. **Leveraging Technology and Analytics:** Using advanced analytics and data-driven insights for continuous monitoring, evaluation, and refinement of sales compensation models, adapting strategies to drive desired sales behaviours effectively.

6. **Transparent Communication:** Ensuring clear and open communication about how compensation structures work,

helping sales teams understand how their efforts translate into rewards.

7. **Flexibility and Adaptability:** Allowing adjustments based on changing market conditions, business strategies, and feedback from the sales team.

8. **Alignment with Corporate Strategy:** Deeply aligning sales compensation plans with the broader strategic goals of the organisation, ensuring sales efforts support overall business objectives.

9. **Focus on Retention:** Offering competitive and appealing compensation packages to retain top talent and maintain a competitive edge in the market.

10. **Cultural Fit:** Designing effective sales compensation strategies that fit well with the company's culture, promoting behaviours and values in harmony with the organisation's ethos.

Assessing Sales Compensation

Sales compensation is a critical lever in driving sales performance and aligning sales strategies with business objectives, but it's also a highly sensitive and potentially combustible area. The design and management of sales compensation plans tread a fine line between motivating the sales force and igniting tensions that can have far-reaching consequences on morale, performance, and retention. Because it directly affects the personal income of sales professionals, making any changes to compensation structures is deeply personal and potentially contentious. Sales personnel's financial planning, lifestyle, and morale are closely tied to expected earnings from commissions and bonuses, making the area of sales compensation highly charged. Any perceived lack of fairness or transparency in how compensation changes are made or communicated can quickly erode trust between sales leadership and the sales force. Changes that make the compensation less attractive than competitors can lead to a talent drain, significantly impacting the organisation's market position and sales performance.

Key Questions for Assessment:

1: Performance-Based Compensation
How does your company use a performance-based compensation model to align sales incentives with strategic business objectives like collaboration? Is the compensation structure actually succeeding in incentivising desired behaviours?

This question assesses the alignment of compensation with company goals, crucial for motivating sales personnel towards activities that directly contribute to business growth. In many instances, the compensation is structured in such a way as to disincentivise desired behaviours.

2: Tiered Commission Structures
Can you describe the tiered commission structure in place at your company and its impact on sales performance?

This explores the motivational aspects of tiered commissions, encouraging sales personnel to exceed targets through progressively higher rewards. It can have the effect of creating envied superstars.

3: Equity-Based Incentives
How do equity-based incentives, if used at all, contribute to aligning the sales team's efforts with long-term company success and retention of top talent?

This question focuses on the role of equity incentives in fostering a sense of ownership among sales staff and their effectiveness in retaining high performers. When companies get this right, the impact can be exponential in effect.

4: Non-Monetary Recognition
What non-monetary recognition programmes exist and what is the feedback like about them?

Great sales organisations are exceedingly good at acknowledging sales achievements beyond financial rewards, celebrating successes and driving up team morale.

5: Impact of Sales Compensation on Team Culture

In what ways has the sales compensation model influenced the culture within your sales team?

Sales compensation has an outsized effect on sales culture including collaboration, competition, and overall morale. When sales compensation is not well done, it has the potential to create enormous dissatisfaction, unhappiness, and can even cause a mass exodus of the best people who seek proper and fair rewards elsewhere.

6: Attraction of Top Talent through Sales Compensation

How does the company's sales compensation structure stand out in attracting the best and brightest talent in a competitive market?

This question aims to uncover the unique elements of the compensation package that make the company an attractive employer for top sales professionals, highlighting the balance between immediate rewards and long-term incentives. Being market-related in compensation does not help matters in the absence of a glittering product or service offering which can temporarily mask mediocre pay structures.

7: Retention Strategies and Commission Staging

What does the staging and timing of commission payments do for the retention of top sales talent, and what are the implications for those considering leaving the company?

Many companies make strategic use of staggered or delayed payments through commission staging as a retention tool, and it is worth exploring how this might create a psychological or financial barrier to leaving, effectively locking in top performers by tying significant portions of their compensation to long-term achievements or company loyalty.

8: Governance and Fair Administration of Sales Compensation

How does your company ensure proper governance in the administration of sales compensation plans, including transparency, consistency, and adherence to policies? Are there causes of concern anywhere?

Proper governance, fair and transparent, is essential not only for maintaining trust and morale within the sales team but also for ensuring that the compensation strategy is implemented as designed, without biases or inconsistencies. One hopes for appropriate documentation and strict adherence to established compensation policies.

9: Balancing Nuance with Simplicity
Does the compensation model strike a balance between sufficient nuance and keeping it simple enough for the sales team to easily understand and be motivated?

A great plan must be sufficiently detailed and nuanced to accurately reflect different levels of sales achievements and behaviours, yet straightforward enough for sales personnel to clearly understand how their actions translate into rewards. The balance between complexity and clarity is crucial for ensuring that the compensation plan effectively motivates desired behaviours without causing confusion or misinterpretation.

10: Integration with Performance Management
How well-integrated is the sales compensation model with the company's overall performance management system, including goal setting, coaching, and feedback processes?

Effective sales compensation should not exist in isolation but should be closely tied to the broader performance management framework. This question investigates the alignment between compensation and other aspects of performance management, ensuring that rewards are not only based on outcomes but also on the behaviours and development of sales personnel.

11. Channel Partnerships

Insights on Channel Partnerships

Channel partners represent the added potential inherent in the channel and ecosystem for market expansion and revenue growth. However, prioritising this area depends on the findings from the diagnostic phase, which assesses the current state and potential of partnerships within the organisation's broader strategic framework. Channel Partners do not always translate into a workstream for turnaround.

Some organisations may have optimally performing channel partnerships, contributing to market reach and revenue without problems. In these cases, optimisation may not be needed and certainly not worth the resources, especially if other areas offer more immediate opportunities. Organisations have limited resources. Deciding to optimise channel partner management means assessing its potential impact compared to other initiatives. If the analysis shows that growth can be better achieved through other means, channel partner management optimisation may not be a priority.

Optimising channel partner management involves complex issues like streamlining onboarding, enhancing portals, clarifying frameworks, and resolving conflicts. If the organisation isn't ready or governed in a way that supports this overhaul, optimisation may be too risky or premature.

The importance and urgency of optimising channel partner management also depend on the market and existing partnerships. In markets where direct sales are more effective or channel conflict is likely, the organisation may focus on strengthening direct customer relationships. If the analysis shows that high-potential partnerships aren't being fully used due to strategic misalignments or inefficiencies, targeted interventions may be more appropriate.

The complexity of channel partner management is underscored by the diversity of commercial arrangements and operational models that govern vendor-partner relationships. These nuances significantly impact the strategy's effectiveness and the overall success of the channel partnerships.

Key considerations include:

- **Type of Channel Partners:** Understanding whether partners are distributors, resellers, agents, or value-added resellers (VARs) is crucial, as each type plays a distinct role and requires different support and incentives.

- **Commercial Arrangements:** The nature of the commercial agreement—whether it involves consignment, buy-resell, or commission-based sales—shapes the dynamics of the partnership, dictating financial flows, risk sharing, and inventory management responsibilities.

- **Collaboration Models:** Sell-To (direct sales to partner), Sell-Through (vendor and partner collaborate), Sell-With (joint sales effort), and Fulfilment Only (partner as delivery arm) models define the level of collaboration and responsibilities in the sales process.

Hallmarks of Excellence in Channel Partner Management

1. **Engagement Level:** Deep engagement with partners across all phases of the customer journey, including joint planning, regular reviews, and collaborative problem-solving.

2. **Incentive Structures:** Tailored incentive programmes that align with both the organisation's goals and the partners' motivations, ensuring attainable and meaningful incentives.

3. **Training and Support:** Extensive product training, sales enablement tools, and marketing support customised to partners' specific needs and market contexts.

4. **Market Coverage and Segmentation:** Strategic allocation of territories and customer segments to partners, optimising market coverage while minimising channel conflict.

5. **Performance Management:** Robust framework for measuring partner performance through relevant metrics and KPIs, facilitating regular performance discussions and identifying areas for improvement.

6. **Technology and Integration:** Seamless integration of partners into the organisation's systems for efficient operations and data sharing.

7. **Compliance and Brand Alignment:** Ensuring partners adhere to the organisation's policies, brand guidelines, and ethical standards through training and monitoring.

8. **Continuous Improvement and Adaptation:** Commitment to ongoing learning, flexibility in strategy and operations, and willingness to pivot to stay ahead of market trends.

9. **Recognition and Rewards for Excellence:** Celebrating and rewarding outstanding partner performance to motivate partners and set benchmarks for success.

10. **Partner Relationship Management (PRM) Software:** Utilising cloud-based PRM software to automate channel management tasks, streamline processes, and provide a centralised platform for collaboration.

11. **Smart Tech and Data-Driven Insights:** Leveraging data analytics, AI, and ML to gain deeper insights into partner performance, customer behaviour, and market trends for targeted programme design and predictive analytics.

12. **Content Co-creation and Personalisation:** Collaborating with partners to create co-branded marketing content that resonates with specific audience segments.

13. **Focus on Customer Experience:** Shifting focus from just selling products to building a seamless customer experience throughout the buyer journey.

14. **Channel Ecosystem Development:** Cultivating a broader ecosystem of partners, including industry influencers, technology partners, and complementary service providers.

Assessing Partners and Channel Programmes

The collaboration models within partner ecosystems reveal a complex tapestry of commercial objectives, engagement strategies, and resource allocations, each tailored to the unique dynamics of the relationship between vendors and their partners.

The "Sell-To" model, involving direct sales to partners such as distributors or wholesalers, necessitates a focus on volume and efficiency, with commercial objectives centred around maximising throughput and minimising friction in the supply chain. This model demands a different engagement and support strategy, primarily focused on logistical and transactional efficiency.

Conversely, the "Sell-Through" model, where vendors and partners collaborate closely to reach the end customer, places a premium on the partner's ability to manage customer relationships and execute sales. Here, the nuances of collaboration revolve around aligning the vendor's and partner's efforts towards seamless customer experiences, requiring shared marketing strategies and customer service philosophies.

The "Sell-With" model represents the epitome of partnership in complex B2B sales environments, necessitating a deep integration of sales strategies, resources, and objectives. This model requires both parties to not only align their commercial goals but also to invest significantly in joint sales training, shared sales intelligence, and coordinated market approaches, reflecting a high degree of mutual dependency and trust.

Lastly, the "Fulfilment Only" model delineates a more transactional relationship, where the partner serves primarily as a logistical extension of the vendor. The commercial objectives here are focused on distribution efficiency and reliability, with less emphasis on sales strategy integration and more on operational excellence and fulfilment capabilities.

Each model delineates distinct paths of collaboration, with varying degrees of engagement, resource sharing, and strategic alignment. Understanding these nuances is crucial for assessment as well as crafting effective partner strategies.

Key Questions for Assessment:

1: Partner Type Integration

How are different types of partners integrated into the overall channel strategy, ensuring a cohesive approach that leverages the unique strengths and capabilities of each partner type?

This question probes the strategic alignment and integration of various partner types within the overarching channel strategy, highlighting the importance of leveraging distinct partner strengths for cohesive market coverage. It underscores the necessity for a nuanced understanding of partner roles and the strategic orchestration of these roles to enhance market reach and effectiveness.

2: Commercials

How effective are the commercial arrangements and agreements in influencing partner behaviour and performance? Are the financial terms clear and unambiguous, and is the deal demarcation managed with fidelity?

The quality and fitness for purpose of commercial agreements reveal much about the dynamics in the partner programme such as the levels of partner engagement, risk-sharing, and overall performance. It is critical to align commercial terms with strategic objectives to foster partner commitment and drive mutual success. The clarity and management of financial terms and deal demarcation is critical for maintaining transparency and trust as fair financial arrangements and robust governance mechanisms prevent disputes and ensure smooth partnership operations.

3: Collaboration Models

Which collaboration models are employed, and how effectively do they align with customer buying preferences and sales objectives?

The alignment between chosen collaboration models and the dual objectives of meeting customer preferences and achieving sales goals is key. The underlying imperatives highlight the importance of selecting collaboration models that not only resonate with customer buying behaviours but also contribute to the strategic sales ambitions of the organisation.

4: Incentive Structures
Are incentive structures optimally designed to motivate desired behaviours and outcomes across different types of partners?

The efficacy of incentive programmes in driving partner behaviours and achieving desired outcomes, such as sales targets and market penetration, needs determination. Carefully crafted incentives must align partner motivations with organisational goals, ensuring the harmonious pursuit of growth.

5: Performance Management
How is partner performance managed, and poor performance corrected, and are the appropriate metrics in place to measure success and identify areas for improvement?

Sales organisations must develop the right mechanisms for monitoring and managing partner performance, focusing on the right metrics to gauge success and guide improvements. This underscores the significance of robust performance management frameworks that enable continuous assessment and enhancement of partner contributions.

6: Customer Centric Execution
Are the channel and the partner agreements constructed to enable selling in a manner preferred by customers, incorporating a multi-channel approach that aligns with customer buying preferences and rhythms?

Alignment between channel partner design and customer buying preferences is critical and this question considers the strategy design in catering to customer needs. All this points to the criticality of customer-centric channel strategies that facilitate seamless buying experiences across preferred touchpoints.

7: Value Creation

Have the collaborations led to demonstrable value creation over time, and are the economic benefits compelling?

Some partner programmes and channel strategies burn resources without ROI. This question evaluates the long-term value and economic benefits derived from channel partnerships, aiming to quantify their impact on the business. It highlights the necessity for partnerships to yield tangible, beneficial outcomes that justify the investment and effort.

8: Partner Relationship Health

Are the channel partnerships healthy and thriving, and are the needs of both the vendor and the channel partners being satisfied?

This question probes the health and mutual satisfaction within channel partnerships, focusing on the balance between vendor and partner needs. It underscores the importance of equitable and productive relationships that foster collaboration and minimise conflict, without which dysfunction will reign supreme.

9: Performance Horizons

How does the organisation ensure an optimal balance between long-term strategic goals and short-term sales performance? Is the performance culture robust enough that, for example, it prioritises hitting monthly targets over speculative big bets?

Balancing short-term sales targets and long-term strategic objectives is challenging. It's crucial to foster growth through strategic partnerships while ensuring these partnerships contribute to immediate financial goals. Leaders must continuously evaluate and adjust partner strategies to effectively support both short-term and long-term objectives. Many organisations focus on speculative, long-term strategies at the expense of immediate financial performance. Developing and reinforcing a commercial mindset that aligns with the need for consistent revenue contributions is essential.

10: Technology and Integration

How seamlessly are partners integrated into our organisation's systems for efficient operations and data sharing? How effectively do we utilise partner relationship management software (PRM) to streamline channel management tasks, improve data analysis, and enhance partner communication?

Utilising cloud-based PRM software is essential for automating tasks, improving efficiency, and providing a centralised platform for collaboration. Providing access to CRM systems, order management tools, and analytics platforms enables partners to operate effectively as an extension of the organisation. Leveraging data analytics and machine learning and AI across all the tech is crucial for predictive insights and informed decision-making, as well as optimising programme performance.

12. Pricing Execution

Insights on Pricing

Pricing strategy and execution are critical to a company's profitability and growth potential. Suboptimal pricing methodologies can wreck a company, while corrections can catalyse major financial improvement. That said, pricing transformation is a very difficult and demanding undertaking.

The B2B space is characterised by complex buyer dynamics and diverse monetisation pathways. Fundamental concepts include price elasticity, value-based pricing, and competitive pricing. Objectives range from maximising short-term revenue to achieving long-term market share growth. Pricing strategies are broadly categorised into market-based and cost-based. Pricing power, the ability to influence price levels, is rare and relies on quantifying value provided to customers.

Understanding the unique needs, preferences, and value drivers of different customer segments is crucial for tailoring pricing strategies and optimising revenue generation. Value-based pricing focuses on the customer's perceived value rather than costs or market prices. Implementing this framework involves identifying customer needs, quantifying differentiated value, nailing the value proposition, and establishing pricing models that reflect value delivered.

Data-driven decision-making is paramount, requiring the collection and analysis of customer price sensitivity, competitor pricing, and cost structures. Advanced analytics techniques can identify trends and patterns to optimise pricing strategies. Effective price setting processes involve methodologies for price discovery, value quantification frameworks, versioning, and bundling.

In complex solution sales, the deal desk manages negotiations, ensures adherence to pricing policies, and allows flexibility for unique customer scenarios. Essential and robust protocols for discounting balance competitiveness with profitability while preventing erosion of value perception among customers. As a colleague once said, "People value what they pay for."

112

Hallmarks of Pricing Execution Excellence

1. **Robust Pricing Strategy:** A well-defined, consistent pricing strategy that aligns with the company's overall objectives and market dynamics. The strategy should be based on a deep understanding of customer value perception, segmentation, and willingness to pay. It should be regularly reviewed and adjusted based on market changes and competitive landscape.

2. **Disciplined Discounting Protocols:** Strict, well-documented discounting policies and approval processes that are consistently enforced across all sales channels. Discounting should be treated as a strategic tool, not a tactical reaction. Clear guidelines on when and how to apply discounts, with a focus on maintaining pricing integrity and preventing margin erosion.

3. **Pricing Governance and Transparency:** A transparent, cross-functional pricing decision-making process that involves key stakeholders from sales, marketing, finance, and product teams. Clearly defined roles and responsibilities for pricing decisions, with regular communication and alignment across departments. Documented pricing policies and change management processes to ensure consistency and accountability.

4. **Value-Based Pricing Orientation:** A pricing approach that focuses on capturing the value delivered to customers, rather than simply covering costs or matching competitors. Extensive customer research to understand value drivers and willingness to pay across different segments. Pricing metrics that align with the value proposition and differentiation of the offering.

5. **Data-Driven Pricing Decisions:** A strong emphasis on market research, competitive intelligence, and data analytics to inform pricing decisions. Regular monitoring of price sensitivity, price elasticity, and transaction prices across different customer segments and channels. Utilisation of advanced analytics tools and techniques to identify pricing opportunities and optimise pricing performance.

6. **Sales Team Pricing Enablement:** Comprehensive training and enablement programmes for sales teams and partners on

value-based selling, pricing communication, and negotiation strategies. Clear pricing guidelines and tools to support the sales process, with a focus on maintaining pricing discipline and consistency. Incentive structures that align with pricing objectives and discourage unauthorised discounting.

7. **Agile Pricing Optimisation:** Continuous monitoring and optimisation of pricing performance based on market feedback, competitive moves, and internal data analysis. Ability to quickly adjust pricing tactics and offerings in response to changing market conditions or customer needs. Regular price-value realisation analysis to ensure that pricing is in line with the value delivered.

8. **Efficient Deal Desk Operations:** A well-structured and efficient deal desk function that supports complex deal negotiations and pricing decisions. Clear deal evaluation criteria and approval processes that balance speed and discipline. Close coordination with sales, finance, and legal teams to ensure compliance and minimise revenue leakage. Continuous improvement of deal desk processes and tools based on performance metrics and feedback.

Assessing Pricing Execution

Transitioning to a new pricing model poses inherent risks both internally, within the company, and externally, with valued clients who may find the change confusing or threatening. Internally, the shift can disrupt established processes, affecting billing systems, sales strategies, and financial forecasting. It necessitates retraining staff to understand and advocate for the new model, which can lead to resistance if not managed properly. Externally, clients accustomed to the previous pricing structure may view the change with scepticism, fearing increased costs or complexity, which could erode trust and satisfaction.

To mitigate the risks, engage in transparent communication to clearly articulate the change's rationale to both staff and clients, highlighting benefits and addressing concerns upfront. Provide comprehensive training to equip employees with the knowledge and tools needed to confidently support and sell the new model, ensuring effective client query resolution. Offering client support through resources like guides, FAQs, and dedicated channels, along with tailored communication, can ease transition concerns. Additionally, considering trial periods through pilot programmes or with a subset of clients allows for real-world feedback and necessary adjustments before a full rollout, ensuring a smoother transition for all parties involved.

Key Questions for Assessment:

1: Pricing Strategy Consistency

How frequently do you observe discrepancies between list and transaction prices, and what impact does this have on your pricing strategy's consistency? To what extent are discounting policies consistently applied across all sales channels? Can discounting be described as a problem and if so, why is it occurring?

It is mission critical that sales organisations maintain pricing integrity and ensure that the pricing strategy is reflective of market dynamics and internal objectives. Uniformity and fairness in the application of discounting policies are crucial for preserving brand value and customer trust. Inconsistent discounting erodes margins, creates channel conflict, and damages the brand. Best-in-class companies have clear guidelines and approval processes for discounts. They also closely monitor transaction prices against list prices to identify issues early. Technology solutions can help enforce discount policies across channels.

2: Pricing Decisions Visibility

How good is the visibility into the company's pricing decisions and the effectiveness of inter-departmental communication regarding pricing strategies?

The focus here is on the transparency of pricing decisions and the efficiency of communication between departments, which are essential for a cohesive pricing strategy unless chaos overwhelms sales operations. Siloed decision making and poor communication lead to misalignment and conflicting actions in the market. Pricing decisions should involve key stakeholders and be clearly communicated. Regular cross-functional meetings on pricing keep everyone informed. Documented pricing policies and change management processes are hallmarks of excellence. Pricing should be recognised as a strategic capability that spans functions.

3: Pricing Strategy and Customer Perception
How well does the pricing strategy align with the perceived value of products/services across different customer segments?

This question addresses the alignment between pricing and customer value perception, a key factor in customer satisfaction and loyalty. If there is much distance between the two, erosions will occur. Prices need to reflect the value delivered to each segment. Extensive customer research is required to understand value drivers. Value-based pricing is the gold standard – it captures a fair share of value.

4: Investment in Market Research
Is the investment in market research and data analytics adequate to ensure accurate customer segmentation for pricing purposes?

The sufficiency of investment in market research and analytics for effective customer segmentation is fundamental for targeted and reliable pricing strategies. Under-investment here leads to a one-size-fits-all approach that leaves money on the table.

5: Data Analytics Utilisation
How good is the utilisation of data analytics in making informed pricing decisions and the adequacy of tools and capabilities for analysing trends to inform our pricing strategy?

The effectiveness of data analytics in pricing decisions and the availability of analytical tools, are critical for adapting to market trends. Data-driven pricing separates the good from the bad and the leaders from laggards.

6: Training and Incentives
How good is the training provided to sales teams and partners on the pricing strategies, and are the incentives for sales teams aligned with the pricing objectives?

Training sales teams and partners on pricing strategies and aligning their incentives with pricing objectives is crucial for ensuring consistent messaging, preventing unauthorised discounting, focusing on value over price, incentivising the right behaviours, enabling value-based selling, and supporting price increases. Effective training provides the sales team and partners with the knowledge and skills to implement pricing strategies as intended, while aligned incentives motivate them to adhere to the desired approach, both of which are necessary for the success of pricing strategies.

7: Competitive Pricing Analysis
How regularly and with what degree of intensity and focus do we conduct competitive pricing analysis and are we agile at adjusting our pricing strategies in response?

Competitive pricing analysis and the ability to respond fast is vital for maintaining market competitiveness. Companies that don't have this capability can lose significant market share and never know why. World-class organisations monitor competitors' prices in real-time.

8: Deal Desk Operations Efficiency
How strong are our Deal Desk operations in terms of dealing with outliers, speeding up sales cycles and closing tricky deals to improve pricing efficiency?

The effectiveness of Deal Desk operations and the coordination with other teams is important for streamlining sales processes and pricing efficiency. High-performing deal desks balance speed and discipline.

9: Opportunities for Pricing Execution Improvement
What are the biggest opportunities for improvement in the pricing execution?

This invites insights into potential areas for enhancing pricing execution and strategy, fostering continuous improvement. There is always room for improvements to be found.

PART TWO | DIAGNOSE

Chapter 6: Collaborating Alliances

Insights on Collaborating Alliances

Establishing robust alliances across the teams in the sales engine is paramount for companies striving to accelerate growth and ensure customer satisfaction. These essential internal collaborations create an environment where strategic alignment, operational efficiency, and seamless customer interactions are harmonised across the customer journey.

Within this ecosystem, the synergy between product development and sales ensures that product offerings are continually refined to meet shifting market demands and customer needs. Presales is a critical link between sales and potential customers, providing in-depth product knowledge and solution customisation that bridges the gap from interest to purchase. The alignment between marketing and sales is crucial for crafting and disseminating a cohesive value proposition that effectively attracts and converts potential leads into engaged customers. Lead generation acts as the initial touchpoint in the customer acquisition process, identifying and nurturing potential leads through targeted outreach and engagement strategies. Following a sale, the collaboration between sales and customer success becomes paramount in fostering customer loyalty and identifying opportunities for additional revenue through strategic retention and upselling efforts. Channel partner management works to build and maintain relationships with resellers, distributors, and other partners to effectively reach and serve a broader customer base.

By advancing beyond merely open lines of communication and strategic cooperation, organisations must pursue strategic and tactical alignment, integration of goals and incentives, and harmonised workflows across these vital functions. It demands a concerted effort to synchronise the diverse operational rhythms and incentive structures of each department.

1. The Product and Sales Alliance

In the competitive landscape of B2B companies, the symbiosis between product development and sales functions is crucial for sustained business growth and customer satisfaction. Superior product lifecycle management (PLM) significantly impacts sales, forming the foundation of success. It ensures products are developed, managed, and retired in alignment with market needs and business objectives. PLM offers a structured framework for managing the changes a product undergoes from inception to retirement, providing sales teams with critical visibility into the product roadmap, enabling them to sell more effectively and strategically.

Superior PLM facilitates a deep understanding of the product's features, benefits, and unique selling propositions (USPs) across its lifecycle. This knowledge is crucial for sales teams, enabling them to accurately and compellingly communicate the product's value to potential customers. Visibility into the product roadmap allows sales teams to align their strategies with the product's development stages, tailoring their pitches to highlight upcoming features or enhancements and managing customer expectations effectively.

Moreover, superior PLM, coupled with visibility into the product roadmap, empowers sales teams to identify and target the most promising market segments and customer profiles. Understanding the product's evolution trajectory enables sales teams to better match the product's capabilities with the specific needs and pain points of different customer segments, enhancing the relevance and appeal of the product to potential buyers.

The insights gained from a well-managed product lifecycle can inform and refine sales strategies over time. Feedback from sales interactions regarding customer needs, market trends, and competitive dynamics can be fed back into the PLM process, fostering a cycle of continuous improvement. This feedback loop ensures product development is responsive to market demands, and sales strategies are informed by up-to-date product knowledge.

The strategic integration of PLM and sales efforts enhances the company's ability to innovate and stay ahead of the competition. By aligning product development with sales strategies, companies can more effectively leverage their product offerings to capture market opportunities and address emerging challenges, maintaining their competitive edge and achieving sustainable growth.

Hallmarks of Excellence in the Product and Sales Alliance

1. **Seamless Communication:** Superior, bidirectional communication between product development and sales teams ensures sales personnel are always equipped with the latest information about product features, updates, and roadmaps, fostering a culture of collaboration and mutual understanding.

2. **Strategic Alignment:** The strategic alignment of the product roadmap with sales objectives ensures product development is closely tied to market demands and sales goals, enhancing the organisation's ability to anticipate market shifts and adapt its offerings.

3. **Customer-Centric Innovation:** A shared commitment to customer-centric innovation leverages insights from sales interactions to inform product development, enhancing product-market fit and strengthening customer relationships.

4. **Proactive Market Engagement:** Early visibility into the product roadmap allows sales teams to prepare the market for upcoming releases and innovations, building anticipation and demand for new features and products.

5. **Integrated Training and Enablement:** Robust lifecycle management ensures sales personnel receive training on new products and features, as well as ongoing enablement resources, enhancing sales effectiveness and customer engagement.

Assessing the Effectiveness of the Product and Sales Alliance

1: Process and Documentation
How is the product lifecycle currently managed and documented? What tools and platforms are used for PLM, and how effective are they in providing visibility and control?

Understanding the existing product lifecycle management (PLM) processes, documentation, and tools helps identify areas for improvement in terms of visibility, control, and efficiency.

2: Cross-Functional Collaboration
Describe the involvement of cross-functional teams in the PLM process and the communication flow between product development, marketing, sales, and customer service teams.

Assessing the level of cross-functional collaboration and communication is crucial for identifying gaps and opportunities to enhance alignment and synergy between teams.

3: Market and Customer Feedback Integration
How is customer and market feedback integrated into the PLM process? Are formal mechanisms in place for capturing and acting on customer insights?

Evaluating the effectiveness of incorporating customer and market feedback into product development helps ensure that products meet evolving customer needs and market demands.

4: Alignment and Communication
To what extent are the product and sales teams aligned on the product roadmap and sales strategies? What channels and frequencies of communication are established?

Assessing the alignment and communication between product and sales teams is essential for identifying areas where misalignment may hinder effective product positioning and sales performance.

5: Sales Enablement and Support
How are new product features and updates communicated to the sales team? What sales enablement resources are provided?

Evaluating the effectiveness of sales enablement and support helps identify gaps in equipping the sales team with the necessary knowledge and resources to effectively sell products.

6: Feedback Loop

Is there a formal process for sales to provide feedback on product features, customer reactions, and competitive positioning? How is sales feedback incorporated into product development, both by the internal teams and the customer?

Assessing the robustness of the feedback loop between sales and product development, and the customer and product development, is crucial for ensuring that real-world customer insights and competitive intelligence inform product enhancements.

7: Visibility and Accessibility

Where could visibility into the PLM process be improved? How accessible is PLM information to all relevant stakeholders?

Identifying areas where visibility and accessibility of PLM information can be enhanced helps streamline communication and decision-making across teams.

8: Communication and Collaboration

What are the main challenges in communication and collaboration between product and sales teams? How could these be improved?

Identifying the key obstacles in communication and collaboration between product and sales teams is essential for developing targeted strategies to enhance alignment and synergy. Assume there will be work to be done to align.

9: Sales Enablement

Are there specific areas where sales enablement could be enhanced? What additional resources or tools do sales representatives need?

Few sales organisations are entirely satisfied with their enablement. Assessing the specific needs and gaps helps prioritise improvements in equipping the sales team with the necessary knowledge, skills, and resources.

10: Metrics and Performance Tracking

What key metrics are used to measure the success of the product and sales alliance? How are these metrics tracked, analysed, and acted upon?

Establishing clear, measurable metrics is essential for objectively evaluating the performance of the product and sales alliance. These metrics may include sales revenue, customer satisfaction scores, product adoption rates, time-to-market, and more. It's crucial to have a robust system in place for tracking these metrics, regularly analysing the data, and using the insights to drive continuous improvement efforts.

2. The Marketing and Sales Alliance

The fusion of marketing and sales disciplines is imperative for achieving enduring growth and enhancing customer engagement. Marketing strategies and sales efforts should be harmoniously aligned with both market demands and organisational goals. This alliance facilitates a comprehensive approach to customer engagement, leveraging insights from both fields to optimise the customer journey and drive revenue growth.

The integration of marketing and sales enables a unified understanding of the customer's needs, preferences, and pain points, crucial for crafting compelling messages and value propositions. Moreover, the alignment between marketing strategies and sales tactics ensures that the customer receives a consistent and personalised experience at every touchpoint. Marketing generates leads by creating targeted content and campaigns, which sales follow up on with tailored solutions, thereby enhancing conversion likelihood.

This collaboration empowers sales teams with rich, data-driven insights into customer behaviour and market trends, gleaned from marketing's analytical capabilities. It allows sales representatives to engage more effectively with prospects, positioning solutions that align with the customer's business objectives. Additionally, the marketing and sales alliance plays a pivotal role in identifying and nurturing key accounts and segments, maximising return on investment and fostering long-term customer loyalty.

Marketing supports opportunity management and deal execution by delivering the right collateral and insights at precisely the right moments in the customer's buying journey, corresponding closely to the sales cycles. This strategic timing ensures that sales teams are equipped with highly relevant and persuasive materials that address the specific concerns and interests of prospects at each stage of their decision-making process.

The feedback loop enriches the strategic planning process, fostering a culture of continuous improvement. Insights from sales interactions inform marketing strategies, ensuring campaigns are responsive to real-world feedback and market dynamics.

Hallmarks of Excellence in the Marketing and Sales Alliance

1. **Unified Customer Insights:** Synthesising and leveraging customer insights across both marketing and sales ensures all interactions are informed by a deep understanding of the customer's business context.

2. **Strategic Cohesion:** The strategic cohesion between marketing campaigns and sales initiatives generates high-quality leads that align with sales priorities, while sales feedback refines marketing strategies.

3. **Content and Messaging Synergy:** A synergy between the content and messaging developed by marketing and the narratives used by sales ensures customers receive a consistent value proposition.

4. **Agile Response to Market Dynamics:** Rapidly adapting strategies and tactics in response to market changes maintains relevance and competitiveness.

5. **Comprehensive Enablement:** Equipping sales teams with the knowledge, tools, and resources to effectively communicate the value of solutions is essential. This includes access to marketing materials, case studies, and data insights.

6. **Precision-Timed Marketing Support:** Delivering highly relevant collateral and insights at critical moments in the customer's buying journey, synchronised with the sales cycle,

ensures sales teams are armed with effective tools to guide prospects towards a favourable decision.

Assessing the Marketing and Sales Alliance

1: Integrated Strategy Development
How are marketing strategies and sales objectives co-developed and aligned to ensure mutual reinforcement and goal achievement?

Assessing the level of integration and alignment between marketing and sales strategies is crucial for ensuring cohesive and effective efforts towards common goals.

2: Precision-Timed Marketing Support
What is the process for identifying and capitalising on critical moments in the customer's buying journey with targeted marketing support?

Evaluating the effectiveness of delivering highly relevant marketing collateral and insights at precise moments in the sales cycle helps ensure sales teams are equipped to guide prospects towards favourable decisions.

3: Cross-Functional Communication
What mechanisms, meetings, and cadences are in place to facilitate regular and effective communication between marketing and sales teams?

Assessing the robustness of cross-functional communication channels and processes helps identify areas for improvement in collaboration and information sharing.

4: Data Sharing and Utilisation
How is customer data integrated and utilised across marketing and sales to inform strategies and decision-making?

Evaluating the effectiveness of data sharing and utilisation practices helps ensure that customer insights are leveraged to drive informed strategies and decisions.

5: Content and Messaging Alignment
How are marketing content and sales messaging consistently aligned across all customer touchpoints?

Assessing the consistency and alignment of content and messaging across marketing and sales helps ensure a unified value proposition is communicated to customers.

6: Lead Generation and Nurturing
How does marketing contribute to lead generation, and what strategies are in place to nurture leads at various stages of readiness?

Evaluating the effectiveness of marketing's lead generation and nurturing efforts helps identify areas for improvement in attracting and engaging high-quality leads.

7: Performance Measurement
What metrics or indicators are used to measure the impact of the marketing and sales alliance, particularly focusing on precision-timed marketing support?

Assessing the robustness of performance measurement practices helps ensure that the impact of the marketing and sales alliance is accurately gauged and optimised.

8: Feedback Mechanisms and Continuous Improvement
How are feedback mechanisms structured to capture insights from sales on the effectiveness of marketing support, and how are these insights used for continuous improvement?

Evaluating the effectiveness of feedback loops and continuous improvement processes helps ensure that insights from sales are leveraged to enhance marketing support.

9: Sales Enablement
How are sales teams trained and enabled to effectively utilise marketing collateral and insights at precise moments in the sales cycle?

Assessing the robustness of sales enablement practices helps identify areas for improvement in equipping sales teams with the knowledge and resources needed to leverage marketing support effectively.

10: Asset Quality and Accessibility

How efficient is marketing at providing sales with the exact assets and insights they need at any given stage in the sales cycle, and if this is self-serve, how good are those assets?

Evaluating the quality, relevance, and accessibility of marketing assets helps ensure that sales teams have the necessary resources to effectively progress opportunities at each stage of the sales cycle.

3. The Sales and Lead Generation Alliance

The Sales and Lead Generation Alliance, although critical for driving business growth and customer acquisition, often faces challenges due to misaligned expectations and objectives. Sales teams frequently question lead quality, while lead generation teams argue that sales do not pursue leads with sufficient dedication. Overcoming these challenges is crucial for the alliance's success.

At its core, the alliance thrives on a deep, symbiotic relationship between generating leads and closing sales. This integration creates a feedback loop where sales insights inform lead generation strategies, ensuring targeted marketing efforts. In turn, sales strategies are refined based on lead quality and behaviour, enabling tailored approaches for different prospect segments.

Hallmarks of Excellence

1. **Enhanced Lead Qualification Processes:** Rigorous lead qualification ensures only high-quality leads are passed to sales.

2. **Transparent Communication and Shared KPIs:** Shared KPIs and regular communication align goals and expectations, fostering transparency and collaboration.

3. **Joint Strategy Development Sessions:** Joint sessions promote mutual understanding and alignment of strategies and objectives.

4. **Feedback Loops and Continuous Training:** Structured feedback and training enhance lead quality and follow-up effectiveness.

5. **Leveraging Technology for Better Integration:** Technology solutions enable better integration, streamlining processes and improving lead tracking.

Assessing the Marketing and Lead Generation Alliance

1: Aligned Strategies and Objectives

Are sales and lead generation strategies and workflows integrated, with clear, unified objectives aligned with business goals?

Assessing the alignment of strategies, workflows and objectives between sales and lead generation is crucial for ensuring cohesive efforts towards common business goals.

2: Customer Insights and Personalisation

To what extent do strategies incorporate deep customer insights and personas, with personalised engagement for different segments?

Assessing the depth of customer understanding and personalisation efforts helps ensure that strategies resonate with the target audience and drive meaningful engagement.

3: Data-Driven Optimisation

How are data analytics used to inform and refine strategies, with processes for continuous optimisation based on performance?

Evaluating the effectiveness of data utilisation and optimisation practices helps ensure that strategies are continuously refined based on real-world performance insights.

4: Technology and Automation

What technologies and automation tools support sales and lead generation, and are there gaps impacting efficiency or effectiveness?

Assessing the robustness of the technology infrastructure helps identify opportunities for leveraging automation and tools to enhance the performance of the alliance.

5: Lead Quality and Nurturing
How are high-quality leads defined and prioritised, and how effective are lead nurturing programmes in guiding prospects?

Evaluating the effectiveness of lead qualification and nurturing practices helps ensure that resources are focused on the most promising opportunities and that prospects are effectively guided towards conversion.

6: Seamless Lead Handoff
Is lead handoff seamless, and how is the quality and timing of these handoffs monitored and optimised?

Assessing the effectiveness of lead handoff processes helps identify areas for improvement in ensuring that sales receive high-quality, well-nurtured leads at the optimal time, maximising the chances of successful conversion.

7: Performance Measurement
What shared KPIs and metrics measure the alliance's performance, and how do feedback loops facilitate continuous improvement?

Assessing the robustness of performance measurement and feedback practices helps ensure that the alliance is held accountable to clear, shared metrics and that insights are leveraged for ongoing optimisation.

4. The Sales and Customer Success Alliance

In the contemporary business landscape, the symbiosis between enterprise sales and customer success teams has emerged as a strategic cornerstone for sustainable growth and customer satisfaction. This collaboration transcends traditional departmental silos, fostering a unified approach to customer engagement and value delivery. The strategic importance of this partnership lies in its capacity to leverage the unique strengths of each team to optimise the customer journey, from initial acquisition through to long-term retention and expansion. By aligning the objectives and activities of sales and customer success, organisations can achieve a more holistic understanding of customer needs, tailor their offerings more effectively, and build enduring relationships that drive revenue growth and competitive advantage.

A distinction between sales and customer success lies in the exchange of value and the fulfilment of promises made to the customer. While both teams are jointly responsible for ensuring the delivery of value, it is imperative that customer success assumes accountability for the fulfilment of these promises. This principle underscores the unique role of customer success in overseeing the customer's journey post-sale, ensuring that the expectations set and promises made by the sales team are met and exceeded.

Traditional account management roles sometimes fall under Customer Success. It is also true that some companies collapse the functions where customer success execs are also opportunity owners. I prefer seeing customer success operating across all accounts, both new and existing, without being opportunity owners.

Hallmarks of Excellence

1. **Integrated Goals:** Integrating team objectives with performance metrics is essential for excellence, focusing on shared goals like improving Net Promoter Score (NPS) and renewal rates. Sales and customer success collaborate closely, ensuring seamless transitions and sustained satisfaction, linking team performance to business impact through a unified customer-centric vision.

2. **Tactical Alignment:** High-performing teams achieve tactical alignment through cross-functional initiatives, including regular joint planning sessions. This ensures strategic and operational synchronisation, moving beyond shared goals to implement strategies that advance the customer journey in a harmonised manner.

3. **Value Exchange:** Excellence entails consistently delivering promised value throughout the customer lifecycle, with a seamless transition from sales to customer success. Success is measured by the customer's perception of value, aligning with or surpassing initial expectations.

4. **Growth Metrics:** Key indicators of success include strong growth within customer accounts, driven by strategic upsell and cross-sell initiatives. Sales and customer success teams collaborate to identify opportunities based on customer needs, monitored through metrics like account expansion rate and year-over-year growth.

5. **Retention and Churn:** Effective collaboration leads to high retention rates and low churn, achieved through proactive engagement, regular health checks, and prompt issue resolution. Data-driven retention strategies utilise insights from customer interactions and satisfaction surveys to prevent churn.

6. **Strategic Upsell/Cross-Sell:** Successful upsell and cross-sell efforts reflect a deep understanding of customer needs, with sales and customer success teams working together to identify value-adding products or features. Coordination ensures these opportunities align with customer objectives and timing.

7. **Communication and Planning:** Successful collaboration is underpinned by excellent communication and tactical alignment, integrating planning and execution across teams. Regular communication and joint planning sessions align sales and customer success on customer goals and challenges.

8. **Data-Driven Decisions:** Excellence involves using data analytics to inform strategies, analysing customer usage, feedback, and satisfaction to guide product development, engagement, and targeted upsell or cross-sell initiatives.

5. The Sales and Presale Alliance

The Sales and Customer Success Alliance has emerged as a strategic cornerstone for sustainable growth and customer satisfaction in the contemporary business landscape. This collaboration transcends traditional departmental silos, fostering a unified approach to customer engagement and value delivery. By aligning the objectives and activities of sales and customer success, organisations can achieve a more holistic understanding of customer needs, tailor their offerings more effectively, and build enduring relationships that drive revenue growth and competitive advantage.

A key distinction between sales and customer success lies in the exchange of value and the fulfilment of promises made to the customer. While both teams are jointly responsible for ensuring the delivery of value, it is imperative that customer success assumes accountability for the fulfilment of these promises, overseeing the customer's journey post-sale and ensuring that the expectations set by the sales team are met and exceeded.

Hallmarks of Excellence

1. **Integrated Goals:** Integrating team objectives with performance metrics is essential, focusing on shared goals like improving NPS and renewal rates. Sales and customer success collaborate closely, ensuring seamless transitions and sustained satisfaction, linking team performance to business impact through a unified customer-centric vision.

2. **Tactical Alignment:** High-performing teams achieve tactical alignment through cross-functional initiatives, including regular joint planning sessions. This ensures strategic and operational synchronisation, moving beyond shared goals to implement strategies that advance the customer journey in a harmonised manner.

3. **Value Exchange:** Excellence entails consistently delivering promised value throughout the customer lifecycle, with a seamless transition from sales to customer success. Success is measured by the customer's perception of value, aligning with or surpassing initial expectations.

4. **Growth Metrics:** Key indicators of success include strong growth within customer accounts, driven by strategic upsell and cross-sell initiatives. Sales and customer success teams collaborate to identify opportunities based on customer needs, monitored through metrics like account expansion rate and year-over-year growth.

5. **Retention and Churn:** Effective collaboration leads to high retention rates and low churn, achieved through proactive engagement, regular health checks, and prompt issue resolution. Data-driven retention strategies utilise insights from customer interactions and satisfaction surveys to prevent churn.

6. **Strategic Upsell/Cross-Sell:** Successful upsell and cross-sell efforts reflect a deep understanding of customer needs, with sales and customer success teams working together to identify value-adding products or features. Coordination ensures these opportunities align with customer objectives and timing.

7. **Communication and Planning:** Successful collaboration is underpinned by excellent communication and tactical alignment, integrating planning and execution across teams. Regular communication and joint planning sessions align sales and customer success on customer goals and challenges.

8. **Data-Driven Decisions:** Excellence involves using data analytics to inform strategies, analysing customer usage, feedback, and satisfaction to guide product development, engagement, and targeted upsell or cross-sell initiatives.

Assessing the Sales and Customer Success Alliance

1: Shared Objectives Alignment
How are sales and customer success teams collaboratively setting and monitoring shared objectives, such as NPS improvement and renewal rates, to ensure alignment with the overarching customer-centric vision?

Assessing the alignment of shared objectives helps ensure that both teams are working towards common customer-centric goals and measuring success consistently.

2: Joint Planning Sessions

In what ways do regular joint planning sessions contribute to strategic and operational alignment between teams, and how do these sessions facilitate the advancement of the customer journey?

Evaluating the effectiveness of joint planning sessions helps identify areas for improvement in fostering collaboration, alignment, and customer-centric strategies.

3: Seamless Transition and Value Delivery

Can you describe the process ensuring a seamless transition from sales to customer success, and how is the delivery of the value proposition tracked and measured against customer expectations?

Assessing the effectiveness of the transition process and value delivery tracking helps ensure that customers receive a consistent, high-quality experience throughout their journey.

4: Growth Opportunity Identification and Execution

How are growth opportunities within customer accounts identified and acted upon, and which metrics are pivotal in monitoring these initiatives for strategic upsell and cross-sell activities?

Evaluating the effectiveness of growth opportunity identification and execution helps ensure that both teams are proactively driving customer success and revenue growth.

5: Proactive Retention Strategies

What proactive engagement strategies are in place to maintain high retention rates and minimise churn, and how are data-driven insights from customer interactions used to inform these strategies?

Assessing the robustness of proactive retention strategies helps identify areas for improvement in leveraging customer insights to drive long-term success and loyalty.

6: Communication and Integrated Planning

Could you detail the mechanisms that facilitate effective communication and integrated planning between sales and customer success, ensuring both teams are synchronised on customer goals and challenges?

Assessing the robustness of communication and integrated planning mechanisms helps identify areas for improvement in fostering seamless collaboration and customer-centric strategies.

7: Data-Driven Decision Making

How is customer data analysed to inform strategic decisions, and what role does this analysis play in guiding product development, customer engagement, and targeted upsell or cross-sell initiatives?

Evaluating the effectiveness of data-driven decision-making helps ensure that strategies and initiatives are informed by actionable customer insights.

8: Metrics for Success

What qualitative and quantitative metrics are most indicative of the collaboration's success, and how are these metrics used to assess and improve team alignment, communication effectiveness, and cross-functional initiatives?

Assessing the relevance and utilisation of success metrics helps ensure that the collaboration is consistently measured, optimised, and aligned with customer-centric goals.

6. The Sales and Channel Partner Management Alliance

The Sales and Channel Partner Management Alliance, while often beset by challenges, is a crucial relationship within most mature organisations. The dynamics between Sales Managers and Channel Partner Managers frequently fluctuate between grudging cooperation and collaboration, stemming from fundamental differences in focus, objectives, incentives, and operational paradigms.

Sales primarily focuses on direct transactions with end-users, striving to meet individual sales benchmarks and quotas.

In contrast, Channel Partner Managers cultivate and oversee relationships with intermediaries to indirectly engage customers, emphasising partner enablement and support. This divergence in focus necessitates an all-out effort to ensure a collaborative relationship, with both teams aligning on overarching goals but pursuing them through distinct avenues and strategies.

The nature of the often-tense relationship is further underscored by the direct versus indirect stewardship of customer relationships. Sales Managers maintain direct customer interactions, while Channel Partner Managers indirectly influence these relationships through intermediaries. The relationship also mirrors a balance between autonomy and alignment, with both roles exercising independence in achieving objectives while cooperating at strategic points to ensure collective success.

Divergent objectives and incentive structures can exacerbate tensions between internal sales teams and channel partners. For example, internal sales may prioritise swift deal conclusions for immediate value, while channel partners may focus on comprehensive solutions with longer sales cycles but sustained revenue potential. Conflicting incentives can lead to situations where short-term sales are favoured over strategic relationship-building.

Hallmarks of Excellence

1. **Creating Aligned Incentive Structures:** Devise compensation models that motivate both teams to strive towards common objectives.

2. **Enhancing Communication and Transparency:** Implement shared platforms and regular strategy meetings to ensure synchronisation on customer needs, pricing, and deal status.

3. **Streamlining Lead Management Processes:** Establish definitive criteria for lead qualification and distribution, allocating leads to the best-equipped party.

4. **Clarifying Rules Around Opportunity Ownership:** Develop explicit guidelines for managing and crediting opportunities, especially when both teams have legitimate claims.

5. **Balancing Data Sharing with Security:** Formulate data governance policies that permit necessary information sharing while protecting sensitive data.

Assessing the Sales and Channel Partner Alliance

1: Goal Alignment
To what extent are the goals and objectives of the Sales and Channel Partner Management teams aligned, and how are potential conflicts in priorities and strategies addressed?

Assessing the alignment of goals and objectives is crucial to ensure they are working towards common organisational aims, despite their distinct focus areas and approaches.

2: Collaboration Effectiveness
How effectively do Sales Managers and Channel Partner Managers collaborate on key initiatives, and what mechanisms are in place to facilitate this collaboration?

Evaluating the effectiveness of collaboration helps identify areas for improvement in leveraging their unique strengths and resources to drive collective success.

3: Incentive Alignment
How well-aligned are the incentive structures for Sales Managers and Channel Partner Managers, and do they encourage behaviours that support the overall goals of the alliance?

Evaluating the alignment of incentive structures is crucial to ensure that both teams are motivated to work together effectively and avoid actions that may undermine the partnership.

4: Communication Channels
How effective are the communication channels and cadences between Sales and Channel Partner Management in facilitating information sharing, feedback loops, and joint problem-solving?

Assessing the effectiveness of communication channels helps identify areas for improvement in ensuring both teams have access to the information and insights they need to work together successfully.

5: Partner Enablement

To what extent does the Sales team support Channel Partner Managers in enabling partners through training, resources, and tools, and how is the effectiveness of these enablement efforts measured?

Evaluating the level and impact of partner enablement support from Sales helps ensure that Channel Partner Managers have the necessary resources to drive partner success and contribute to the alliance's goals.

6: Customer Experience Coordination

How well-coordinated are the efforts of Sales and Channel Partner Management in delivering a seamless and consistent customer experience across direct and indirect channels?

Assessing the coordination of customer experience efforts helps identify opportunities to improve alignment and ensure customers receive a high-quality experience regardless of the channel.

7: Data and Insights Sharing

How effectively do Sales and Channel Partner Management teams share data and insights related to market trends, customer needs, and competitive landscape, and how is this information leveraged to inform joint strategies?

Evaluating the sharing and utilisation of data and insights helps ensure that both teams have a comprehensive understanding of the market and can make informed decisions that benefit the alliance as a whole.

Cooperating Partnerships

The cooperative relationships between sales and various other functions within an organisation, such as Finance, Human

Resources (HR), Information Technology (IT), Professional Services, Project Management, Legal, and Operations, are vital for the operation and success of a business. However, these relationships are more accurately described as cooperating teams rather than collaborating alliances given the dynamics and operational frameworks that govern these interactions.

The distinction should be clarified. Collaboration involves parties jointly working towards shared goals, often creating outcomes together, merging their resources and efforts to achieve a common objective that they couldn't achieve alone. In contrast, cooperation sees parties with separate goals assisting each other, driven by mutual benefits.

Cooperating Teams vs. Interdependent Collaborating Alliances

Cooperating teams have goals and objectives that align and can even be shared, but maintain distinct responsibilities, objectives, and methodologies. Their cooperation is essential for achieving common organisational goals, yet they function independently within their own domains of expertise. Interdependent alliances, on the other hand, suggest a deeper, more symbiotic relationship where the success of one entity directly influences the success of the other, often blurring the lines between their operational boundaries.

Cooperating Role Dynamics

1: Finance and Sales

The relationship between Finance and Sales is characterised by a mutual dependency on shared objectives, such as revenue growth and financial health. However, their operations remain distinct. Their cooperation is essential for balancing profitability with market competitiveness, but they do not share operational functions.

Best Practices for Alignment:

a) Establish regular communication channels on set cadences to discuss financial targets, budgets, and performance metrics.

b) Collaborate on sales forecasting and pipeline management to ensure financial projections are accurate and achievable.
c) Jointly work toward effective pricing execution that balances profitability with market competitiveness and customer value.

2: Human Resources (HR) and Sales
HR and Sales work together to ensure the sales team is well-staffed, highly skilled, and motivated. Some goals are aligned, but their day-to-day operations are independent.

Best Practices for Alignment:

a) Collaborate on defining the ideal salesperson profile, including skills, competencies, and experience.
b) Partner on recruitment and selection processes to identify and attract top sales talent.
c) Jointly develop training and development programmes to enhance sales team capabilities and performance.
d) Work extremely closely to ensure the new hire onboarding process is exemplary.

3: IT and Sales
The sophistication of sales tools and CRM systems necessitates a close relationship between IT and Sales, but their functions and expertise areas remain separate.

Best Practices for Alignment:

a) Involve Sales in the selection and implementation of sales-related technologies to ensure user adoption and effectiveness.
b) Establish service level agreements (SLAs) to ensure IT provides timely and adequate support for sales systems and tools.
c) Collaborate on data management and analytics initiatives to leverage sales data for insights and decision-making.

4: Sales and Professional Services
Professional Services typically supports the implementation and customisation of solutions sold by Sales. While their success is

closely linked, Professional Services operates post-sale, focusing on customer satisfaction and solution effectiveness, distinguishing their role from the sales process.

Best Practices for Alignment:

a) Involve Professional Services in the pre-sales process to ensure proposed solutions are feasible and deliverable.
b) Establish a seamless handoff process between Sales and Professional Services to ensure a smooth transition for customers.
c) Share customer feedback and insights between Sales and Professional Services to continuously improve solution offerings and delivery.

5: Sales and Legal

The cooperation between Sales and Legal is fundamental in navigating contracts and regulatory compliance. Legal advises and safeguards the company's interests, enabling Sales to focus on customer engagement within the bounds of legal and ethical standards. Their efforts ensure compliance and risk management without merging their operational responsibilities.

Best Practices for Alignment:

a) Involve Legal early in the sales process to review and approve contract terms and conditions.
b) Collaborate on developing the most efficient system in order to streamline the contracting process.
c) Provide training to the sales team on legal and compliance issues to mitigate risks.

Legal departments, while crucial for risk management, can inadvertently become significant bottlenecks in deal closure. Their meticulous review processes, essential for protecting company interests, often clash with Sales' urgency to close deals. Robust governance is needed to maintain compliance without sacrificing agility in the sales cycle.

6: Sales and Operations

In organisations dealing with physical products, Sales and Operations work to align product availability with customer demand. Operations manage the supply chain and inventory, supporting Sales' efforts to meet customer needs. In service-based organisations, the cooperation between Sales and Operations is equally critical, focusing on aligning service capacity with customer requirements. Operations ensure the seamless delivery of services sold by the sales team, managing resources, processes, and quality control. While their goals are interconnected, their operational activities are distinct, with Operations focusing on service delivery and optimisation, while Sales concentrates on customer acquisition and relationship management.

Best Practices for Alignment in Product-based Organisations:

a) Establish a robust sales and operations planning (S&OP) process to align demand forecasts with production and inventory plans.

b) Collaborate on setting service level targets for order fulfilment and delivery to meet customer expectations.

c) Share real-time data on sales, inventory, and production to enable quick responses to changes in demand or supply.

Best Practices for Alignment in Service-based Organisations:

a) Jointly develop service level agreements (SLAs) that define the scope, quality, and timeliness of service delivery, ensuring Sales and Operations are aligned on customer commitments.

b) Collaborate on capacity planning to ensure sufficient resources are available to deliver services sold by the sales team.

c) Establish a feedback loop between Sales and Operations to share customer insights, identify improvement opportunities, and enhance service quality.

d) Implement a robust project management framework to coordinate the handoff between Sales and Operations, ensuring seamless service initiation and delivery.

e) Regularly review and optimise service delivery processes to improve efficiency, quality, and customer satisfaction.

Aligning Collaborative Alliances for High Performance

Aligning collaborative alliances for high performance is both an art and a science, requiring a nuanced approach that integrates psychology, facilitation, and business strategy. This process typically takes place during the delivery phase of an engagement but has been included here to flow logically from the preceding section. Mastering this alignment involves harmonising people, processes, technology, and leadership towards a shared goal and set of objectives. The methodology leverages principles from psychology, facilitation training, and advanced business studies to create cohesive and effective alliances. The approach includes meticulous planning and facilitation to ensure all elements work in concert, enabling high performance and strategic alignment. Here's an outline of how this process is facilitated:

1. Conduct an Assessment:

The first step is a comprehensive assessment to understand the current state of affairs. This involves a deep dive into what is working and what isn't, examining the facets of people, processes, technology, communication protocols, and leadership. This stage is critical for identifying misalignments, friction and bottlenecks, and opportunities for enhancement. By employing both quantitative and qualitative analysis methods, actionable insights are gathered to form the foundation for transformative strategies.

2. Summary and Distribution:

Following the assessment, a summary of my findings with key insights, challenges, and potential opportunities for improvement should be documented and distributed to the leaders of the respective teams and the steering committee (SteerCo). This step ensures that all stakeholders are on the same page, fostering a shared understanding of the current state and the need for alignment and turnaround.

3. Schedule Offsite:

With the groundwork laid, the next step is to schedule an offsite. This is not just a meeting, but a strategic retreat to a neutral place designed to foster open dialogue and strategic thinking, away from the day-to-day operations and incessant distractions.

4. Run the Offsite with a Specific Structure:

1. **Theory and Shared Language Creation:** The offsite begins with a theoretical framework that introduces new concepts and methodologies relevant to our goals. Creating a shared language is pivotal for ensuring that all members have a common understanding of the terms, concepts, and frameworks that will be used throughout the alignment process.

2. **Integration Exercises:** Following the theoretical foundation, we engage in integration exercises. These are designed to apply the newly introduced concepts in a practical, hands-on manner, facilitating deeper understanding and integration of the ideas into our working practices. The exercise also bonds the teams and breaks down defensive posturing.

3. **Sharing and Storytelling:** A powerful tool for alignment and motivation, sharing and storytelling sessions allow team members to share their experiences, challenges, and successes. This fosters empathy, understanding, and a sense of shared purpose among the participants.

4. **Vision-Setting:** A key outcome of the offsite is the establishment of a clear, compelling vision for the future. This vision acts as a north star, guiding the turnaround efforts and ensuring that all actions are aligned with the overarching objectives.

5. **Courageous Conversations:** Facilitated and with a given structure, we will have the conversations that matter most to the team, the ones that move the needle because they are so important to the health of the collaboration. Here is where feedback is given and received, the impact of people behaviour is shared and discussed and where resolutions

146

and commitments are made. The air must be fully cleared, grievances resolved and bonds between people restored.

6. **Goals and Objectives Setting:** With a vision in place, we then set goals and objectives. The OKR methodology works best, but SMART goals work well too. This step translates the vision into actionable targets that provide direction and focus for the turnaround efforts.

7. **Workflow Integration and Operational Refinement:** This step involves a detailed analysis and integration of workflows to ensure seamless operations across teams and includes identifying and mapping out key workflows and processes, clarifying interdependencies, fine-tuning workflows and KPIs to measure the effectiveness of integrated workflows and ensure alignment with overall objectives.

8. **Creation of a Collaboration Charter:** The final step in the process and where we agree the purpose of the collaboration, its scope, and the expected outcome, roles and responsibilities, communication protocols and meeting cadences, decision architecture and the mechanisms to ensure continued improvement.

Measures of Success

How does one know that the workshop was a success? It's quite simple:

1. **Comradery, cohesion, and alignment:** there will be a buzz in the air characterised by mutual respect, trust, and a sense of belonging to a real team. The Charter will have been successfully co-created, and everyone will have participated, and had a voice.

2. **Absence of Unspoken Truths and Concealed Facts:** We would have succeeded in establishing a safe and trusting environment where issues were addressed openly and constructively, preventing misunderstandings and fostering a culture of honesty and integrity.

3. **Resolution of Conflicts:** In any collaborative environment, disagreements and conflicts are inevitable, but our success in resolving these issues in a manner that respects all parties' perspectives and strengthens the alliance is what we are aiming for. I have led workshops before as a young facilitator where this did not happen in full, and residual pockets of fragmentation remained even after we concluded.

PART TWO | DIAGNOSE

Chapter 7: Clarifying the Vision

Clarifying the vision, or the revisioning process, is a crucial step in the sales transformation journey. As a change leader, considerable time and effort have been invested in uncovering the problems within the sales engine. Through listening to various perspectives and stories and hearing conflicting views on what is working and what is not, a deeper understanding of the challenges has been gained. Importantly, people within the sales organisation have taken career risks by confiding in the change leader and divulging sensitive information.

The Need

At this juncture in the turnaround journey, a potential Pandora's box of issues, complications, and unknown ramifications may have been unveiled. If the process has been done well, a host of problems, complex interdependencies, and uncertainty around solutions will have been identified. This is an opportune time to pause and envision an optimistic end-state. Revisioning serves several key purposes in the sales transformation process. It provides an opportunity to reset and align the organisation, offers containment and reassurance to those who have shared sensitive information, creates a forum for inspiration and creative energy to flow, and most importantly, builds consensus around what the future must and will look like.

Envisioning a compelling future, free of current constraints, adds necessary fuel and aligns stakeholders on what success looks like across different dimensions. An ambitious vision stretches thinking beyond incremental improvements to bolder departures from the status quo, implying significant changes to strategies, structures, and cultures. Vivid visions instil ownership by allowing each stakeholder to see themselves as protagonists in the future story and provide the guiding star for the journey.

Revisioning in the Context of the Transformation Journey

Revisioning plays a vital role in supporting the entire transformation programme and its various components. It helps to prioritise and focus efforts on the most critical areas for change, provides a shared language and framework for communicating the transformation journey, supports the development of a roadmap, and embeds the transformation ethos into the organisation's psyche.

Principles

To conduct revisioning quickly and effectively, several principles can be employed. Leading with provocative questions in workshop forums sparks imaginative thinking unconstrained by current limitations. Focusing on 'Be' rather than 'Do' articulates vision around identities and provides flexibility. Embracing tensions and allowing space for debate around vision trade-offs sparks creativity. Co-creating the vision by involving as many people as possible drives ownership. Benchmarking the best by infusing visioning with external perspectives expands thinking.

Risks and Mitigation

Given the sensitive nature of the information shared during the transformation journey, there are several risks that must be addressed through effective revisioning. These include individuals feeling exposed or vulnerable, the transformation becoming derailed by competing priorities or a lack of alignment, resistance from frontline sales teams, and leaders losing credibility or authority. By conducting revisioning in a way that provides containment and reassurance, articulating a clear and compelling vision, involving as many people as possible, and showcasing commitment to the transformation, change leaders can mitigate these risks.

The Measures of Success

The success of the revisioning process can be measured by several key indicators, including the level of alignment and consensus around the vision, the degree to which the vision stretches beyond incremental improvements, the extent to which the vision instils ownership and inspires action, and the effectiveness of the vision in guiding decision-making and aligning initiatives towards the desired future state.

Revisioning Workshop Framework

The primary objectives of the revisioning workshop are to align stakeholders around a shared vision of the future sales organisation, identify key priorities and initiatives to achieve the desired future state, and build consensus and commitment to the transformation journey.

The workshop follows an agenda that includes an introduction and context setting, envisioning the future through guided visioning exercises, prioritising initiatives based on impact and feasibility, action planning in small groups, and securing commitments and discussing next steps. The total time for the revisioning workshop is approximately 3 hours, with breaks included to allow participants to recharge and refocus.

Post-workshop follow-up involves synthesising the outputs into a clear, compelling vision statement, refining and finalising the prioritised initiatives and action plans, communicating the vision and initiatives broadly across the organisation, establishing governance structures and feedback loops, and continuously engaging stakeholders to maintain momentum throughout the transformation journey.

PART THREE | DESIGN

Chapter 8: Designing Solutions

Building upon the foundation laid by the Discovery phase, Solution Design is next in the sales turnaround journey. It is mightily consequential, as time, money, and executive patience are finite resources. The actual design translates the insights and recommendations gleaned from the initial analysis into actionable strategies designed to drive meaningful change. The design needs to be pinpoint accurate.

When presenting a transformation design to sponsors and executives after the analysis phase, it's crucial to understand their expectations, preferences, and potential concerns. Here's what they typically want to see, what can delight them, and what might turn them cold.

What sponsors and executives demand, without compromise, is a demonstration of how the proposed transformation design aligns with and supports the organisation's overall strategic goals and priorities. They expect a compelling case for the expected benefits, showcasing quantifiable improvements in KPIs and expected ROI, backed by solid numbers. A data-driven approach, grounded in rigorous analysis, benchmarking, and insights from the analysis phase, is non-negotiable.

Executives want to see a thorough identification of potential risks and challenges, along with a well-thought-out mitigation plan. They need a detailed implementation roadmap with specific milestones, timelines, and responsibilities, demonstrating a well-structured approach. Don't forget the human element; discuss stakeholder engagement and present a robust change management strategy to drive adoption and minimise resistance.

To get executives excited, present innovative yet practical solutions that push boundaries while remaining feasible. Identify opportunities for quick wins and propose a phased implementation approach to maintain momentum. Showcase the incorporation of industry best practices and benchmarking insights to position recommendations as a way to gain a competitive edge. Use engaging visuals, infographics, and storytelling techniques to bring the transformation design to life, creating excitement and buy-in. Demonstrate the design's adaptability to accommodate future growth, changing market dynamics, and evolving strategic priorities.

On the flip side, executives can be turned off by a lack of clarity, specificity, and actionable recommendations. Insufficient data, analysis, or insights to support the proposed design will raise doubts about its validity and potential impact. Underestimating risks, challenges, and barriers to implementation, or misalignment with strategic priorities, will quickly disengage executives. Overly ambitious, impractical, or disconnected recommendations that fail to address the people side of change and present a comprehensive change management strategy will worry executives about the transformation's long-term sustainability and adoption. Showing a lack of understanding of available resources is a surefire way to lose support.

The key is to strike the right balance between vision and practicality, innovation and feasibility, ambition and realism. Present a transformation design grounded in data, aligned with strategic priorities, and supported by a robust implementation and change management plan. Do that, and you'll have executives eating out of the palm of your hand.

Prioritising and Addressing Critical Problems

Before delving into the intricacies of Solution Design, it is essential to take a step back and assess the set of problems identified during the Diagnostic phase. Not all issues are created equal, and it is crucial to prioritise them based on their criticality, impact, and the resources available to address them.

To effectively prioritise problems:

1. Evaluate the consequences of each problem on the organisation's sales performance and overall strategic objectives

2. Assess the potential impact of solving each problem in terms of revenue growth, cost savings, and customer satisfaction

3. Consider the resources required to address each problem, including time, budget, and human capital

4. Rank the problems based on their criticality and potential impact, focusing on those that offer the highest return on investment

5. Align the prioritised problems with the organisation's strategic objectives to ensure a cohesive approach to Solution Design

By prioritising the most consequential problems, organisations can allocate their resources effectively and design solutions that yield the greatest benefits.

Aligning Solutions with Strategic Objectives

At the core of effective Solution Design lies the principle of strategic alignment. Every proposed solution must be meticulously crafted to support and advance the organisation's overarching strategic objectives. This ensures that the transformation efforts are not merely superficial fixes but rather purposeful initiatives that contribute to the realisation of long-term goals.

To achieve this alignment, it is essential to show you have calibrated to the organisation's vision, mission, and strategic priorities. Identify the specific objectives that the sales turnaround aims to achieve, map each proposed solution to the corresponding strategic objective(s), and validate the alignment through stakeholder feedback and consensus-building.

Balancing Innovation and Pragmatism

Solution Design demands a delicate balance between innovation and pragmatism. While it is crucial to push the boundaries and explore novel approaches, it is equally important to ensure that the proposed solutions are feasible and sustainable within the organisation's context.

To strike this balance encourage creative thinking and out-of-the-box ideas during the ideation phase. Assess the viability of each solution based on resource availability, timeline, and budget. Prioritise solutions that offer the optimal trade-off between impact and ease of implementation. And always iterate and refine solutions based on feedback and evolving circumstances.

Engaging Stakeholders for Buy-In and Ownership

The success of any sales turnaround hinges on the active engagement and buy-in of key stakeholders across the organisation. Solution Design presents an invaluable opportunity to involve these stakeholders in shaping the future state, fostering a sense of ownership and commitment to the transformation journey.

To effectively engage stakeholders:

1. Identify the key stakeholders who will be impacted by or have influence over the turnaround deployment and delivery

2. Communicate transparently about the objectives, process, and expected outcomes. Ensure that everyone knows exactly what is expected of them

3. Solicit input and feedback through workshops, interviews, and collaborative sessions

4. Address concerns and incorporate valuable insights into the solution refinement process

5. Continuously update stakeholders on progress and milestones to maintain engagement

Designing for Scalability and Adaptability

In a rapidly evolving business landscape, solutions must be designed with scalability and adaptability in mind. This ensures that the sales transformation can accommodate future growth, changing market dynamics, and technological advancements without requiring significant overhauls. To embed scalability and adaptability into Solution Design, adopt modular and flexible architectures that allow for easy expansion and modification.

Measuring Success and Driving Continuous Improvement

The true test of Solution Design lies in its ability to deliver measurable results and drive continuous improvement. Establishing clear business outcomes and measures of success is essential to gauge the effectiveness of the implemented solutions and identify areas for further optimisation.

Best Practices

Incorporate Design Thinking

Design Thinking provides a valuable framework for Solution Design. This human-centred approach focuses on deeply understanding the needs and challenges of sales teams and customers, defining problems clearly, ideating potential solutions, and rapidly prototyping and testing ideas. By applying Design Thinking principles, one can develop empathy with users, define and frame the right challenges, generate creative ideas, build prototypes, gather feedback, and iterate on designs to better meet user needs. Incorporating Design Thinking into Solution Design can lead to more innovative and user-centric sales strategies, customer engagement models, and enablement approaches. It encourages a culture of experimentation and learning, driving continuous improvement in the sales organisation.

Systems Thinking in Solution Design

It is worth reiterating that sales organisations are complex systems with many interrelated components. Applying Systems Thinking to solution design involves understanding these interconnections and identifying key leverage points for driving change. Map out the complex web of relationships and dependencies within the sales system, identify feedback loops and unintended consequences of potential interventions, and pinpoint high-leverage areas where targeted solutions can have an outsized impact. Design holistic solutions that address root causes rather than surface-level symptoms, anticipating and planning for the ripple effects of changes across the sales organisation.

Addressing Organisational Dynamics

Cultural and Language Considerations in Solution Design

Organisational culture plays a critical role in the success of any sales transformation initiative. Solutions that are not aligned with the prevailing culture or relevant languages may face resistance, low adoption, and limited impact. Effective Solution Design must take cultural factors into account, including values, norms, behaviours, barriers to change, and cultural strengths. The change management plan should be adapted to these nuances as well.

Assess Cultural Readiness and Commercial Maturity

Assessing cultural readiness involves considering dimensions such as risk tolerance, openness to experimentation, propensity for collaboration, and engaging in cross-functional or multicultural teamwork. It's crucial to meet the organisation where it is in terms of its commercial sophistication and capabilities. Before designing solutions, take a hard look at the organisation's current level of commercial maturity and be honest about where they are on the spectrum.

Sustainability and Evolution of Solutions

Sales transformation is an ongoing journey. Designing solutions for sustainability and continuous evolution is critical to maintaining their relevance and effectiveness over time. Key strategies include building in mechanisms for ongoing performance monitoring and analytics, establishing feedback loops, creating governance structures for solution refinement and adaptation, and investing in ongoing training and enablement. A framework for periodic solution review and adaptation could involve quarterly business reviews to assess solution performance, annual strategic planning sessions to align solution roadmaps with business objectives, and partnerships with external experts to infuse fresh perspectives and best practices.

PART THREE | DESIGN

Chapter 9: The Consulting
and Client Teams

The success of a sales turnaround relies on the composition and capability of the consulting team leading the initiative. The ideal team consists of a core group and subject matter experts (SMEs) who collaborate to drive change.

The core team includes:

1. **Consulting/Engagement Leader:** Orchestrates the team, provides executive-level leadership, and ensures client satisfaction.

2. **Account Manager:** Serves as the main client contact and handles commercial aspects.

3. **Account Director:** Oversees the client account and provides counsel to the executive leadership team.

4. **Programme Manager:** Handles day-to-day planning, coordination, and tracking against the turnaround roadmap.

5. **Capability Lead:** Focuses on sales training, designing learning interventions, and competency development.

SMEs are brought in based on the findings from the deep diagnostic phase and align with the contingent workstreams. Each SME brings their unique expertise and perspective:

6. **Technology Lead:** Focuses on optimising the tech stack and ensuring it supports the sales process effectively.

7. **Channel Partner SME:** Seeks to maximise the potential of partnerships and drive growth through indirect sales channels.

8. **Sales Operations SME:** Aims to streamline processes, improve efficiency, and provide actionable insights through data analysis.

9. **Marketing SME:** Strives to align marketing efforts with sales objectives and generate high-quality leads.

10. **Customer Success SME:** Prioritises customer retention, satisfaction, and advocacy to drive long-term growth.

11. **Sales Compensation SME:** Ensures compensation structures are fair, motivating, and aligned with business goals.

12. **Data Analytics and Insights SME:** Leverages data to inform decision-making and identify opportunities for improvement.

13. **Product Management SME:** Aligns product development with market needs and equips sales teams with the right knowledge and tools.

14. **Legal and Compliance SME:** Focuses on minimising legal risks and ensuring adherence to regulations.

15. **Talent Management SME:** Concentrates on attracting, developing, and retaining top sales talent to drive performance.

16. **Pricing SME:** Develops pricing strategies that balance competitiveness, profitability, and customer perception of value.

Measuring Success

Measuring the success of the consulting team involves tracking both quantitative and qualitative metrics. Quantitative metrics include client satisfaction scorecards, milestone tracking, sales performance indicators, and adoption levels. Qualitative metrics encompass stakeholder feedback, collaboration and joint accountability, and cultural and behavioural changes.

Client Stakeholders

The success of the turnaround also depends on the engagement and contributions of client stakeholders, each playing a unique role driven by specific responsibilities, agendas, and critical insights:

1. **Executive Sponsor (usually the CEO):** Focused on overall business growth, market share expansion, and ROI from the turnaround.

2. **Chief Revenue Officer:** Prioritises revenue growth, customer acquisition, and sales efficiency.

3. **Head of Sales:** Concentrates on achieving sales targets, improving conversion rates, and enhancing team performance.

4. **Head of Sales Operations:** Aims to optimise sales processes, improve CRM utilisation, and enhance forecasting accuracy.

5. **Head of Marketing:** Strives to align marketing strategies with sales goals and generate high-quality leads.

6. **Head of Customer Success:** Emphasises customer retention, satisfaction, and expanding lifetime value.

7. **Head of Global (or Strategic Accounts):** Focuses on nurturing and growing key accounts to drive long-term success.

8. **Head of Presales:** Ensures the presales process effectively addresses customer needs and supports sales objectives.

9. **CIO:** Prioritises technology infrastructure scalability, data security, and integration of sales tools.

10. **Client Programme Manager:** Concentrates on keeping the project on track, within budget, and aligned with objectives.

11. **HR Director:** Ensures the best available talent is thriving and aligned with the turnaround goals.

12. **Finance Director:** Provides financial oversight, manages costs, and ensures the turnaround delivers ROI.

13. **Head of Channel Partners:** Seeks to optimise channel partner relationships and drive growth through indirect sales.

Recognising and navigating these diverse agendas and motivations is crucial for the consulting team to effectively collaborate with both SMEs and client stakeholders. By understanding and aligning these various interests, the team can create a cohesive strategy that addresses the unique needs and concerns of each stakeholder while driving the turnaround towards success. The collective efforts of the consulting team and client stakeholders, guided by clear KPIs and priorities, are essential for achieving the desired outcomes of the sales turnaround initiative.

Conflicting Agendas

Conflicting agendas among client stakeholders can pose significant challenges to the success of the initiative. I will say more about this in Alignment and Governance. These conflicts often arise due to differing priorities, KPIs, and perspectives on what constitutes a successful outcome. Here are some common examples of conflicting agendas that can be expected and can derail things derail things if not surfaced and resolved:

1. **Short-term vs. Long-term Goals:** The executive sponsor (CEO) may prioritise the share price and long-term strategic objectives and market share expansion, while the Head of Sales may be more focused on achieving short-term sales targets and quotas. This can lead to tensions around resource allocation and the pace of change implementation.

2. **Revenue Growth vs. Profitability:** The Chief Revenue Officer may push for aggressive revenue growth strategies, such as expanding into new markets or offering discounts to win deals. However, the Finance Director may prioritise profitability and cost management, leading to conflicts around pricing, investment decisions, and the financial viability of certain initiatives.

3. **Marketing vs. Sales Alignment:** The Head of Marketing may advocate for investing in brand-building activities and top-of-funnel lead generation, while the Head of Sales may prefer a more bottom-of-funnel approach focused on closing deals

and converting leads. This can result in disagreements around budget allocation, content creation, and the definition of a qualified lead.

4. **Technology Investment vs. Process Optimisation:** The CIO may champion the adoption of new sales technologies and tools to enhance efficiency and data-driven decision making. However, the Head of Sales Operations may argue that the focus should be on streamlining existing processes and ensuring better utilisation of current systems before investing in new ones.

5. **Customer Acquisition vs. Customer Retention:** The Head of Sales may prioritise acquiring new customers to drive revenue growth, while the Head of Customer Success may emphasise the importance of retaining existing customers and maximising their lifetime value. This can lead to debates around resource allocation, account management strategies, and the relative importance of new vs. existing business.

More on this in the next chapter.

PART FOUR | IMPLEMENT

Chapter 10: Governance and Project Alignment

Insights on Governance and Project Alignment

Project or steering committee (SteerCo) meetings can be taxing, nightmarish even. These forums and the group processes are not easy to manage – they consist of senior, opinionated executives, many egotistical and A-type, and most political by nature. This is quite typical of the corporate world and even more so in the dynamic world of sales revenue generation and the functions in the revenue engine.

In every governance-type meeting you can be guaranteed of a few things:

- **Politics** – everything gets played out in a political 'field'.

- **Power dynamics** – in every group between all the relationships and in every meeting and group process there is an invisible rung and people occupy different places on it, depending on variables like role, seniority, the status of their function, their education, affluence, age, and the list goes on and on......

- **Conflicting agendas** – no group has perfectly aligned goals, objectives and priorities and no group, just like no couple, is perfectly compatible.

- **Personality differences** – there are big ones and small ones and colourful ones in each group and they don't always harmonise.

- **Differences cultures, values, and morals** – each person has their own unique moral and ethical compass.

All of this makes for complexity in human relations, and the person driving the Turnaround needs to be adept at managing these dynamics. All meetings need to be facilitated in such a way as to give everyone a voice, and in ways that leverage the wisdom in the group. This skill alone deserves its own chapter. But, getting back to the fundamentals of governance and alignment there a few things one should ensure:

Institute a Steering Committee (SteerCo) with clear mandates

The steering committee comprising executive sponsors and senior leaders make key decisions and govern strategic direction, budget decisions, and removal of roadblocks. You must define guiding principles, decision authority limits, and the cadence of involvement. Balance unnecessary meddling with adequate oversight.

Empower a Strong Programme Management Office (PMO)

The PMO turns strategy into action through meticulous project planning, risk mitigation, resource allocation, and programme delivery oversight. Provide ample tools, technologies and authority to execute on governance protocols.

Infuse data-driven decision making

Leverage data, analytics and insights to ground decisions. Intuition has its place, but objective data minimises bias and builds confidence in chosen paths especially when navigating ambiguity.

Formulate clear programme reporting protocols

Consistency and discipline in reporting spur alignment. Established templates, cadence, channels and meeting rhythms provide touchpoints for assessing progress, identifying deviations, and correcting course.

Aligning the Players

Managing and aligning project teams, particularly in the context of complex initiatives like sales turnarounds, demands very high emotional acuity and a very nuanced approach that fosters cohesion, drives high performance, and effectively manages conflict. The principles I will share will stand you in good stead for achieving strategic alignment among project stakeholders, ensuring that the collective efforts are harmonised towards the common goal of turnaround.

*Define roles and responsibilities and
eradicate ambiguity from day one*

Clarity is the cornerstone of team alignment. Utilising RACI charts to delineate who is Responsible, Accountable, Consulted, and Informed eliminates doubt and sets clear expectations. This foundational step ensures that each team member understands their role in the project's ecosystem, fostering accountability and streamlining communication. Fail here and a world of pain awaits.

Schedule alignment meetings on a regular cadence

The dynamic nature of sales Turnarounds necessitates frequent touchpoints. Both formal steering committee meetings and informal gatherings serve as platforms for discussing progress, addressing concerns, and reinforcing the project's vision. These meetings are vital for maintaining momentum and ensuring that all team members are aligned with the project's objectives. SteerCo meetings should be held at least two times a month together with weekly meetings with teams, task group etc.

Build solid feedback channels

Open lines of communication are essential for capturing stakeholder sentiments. Promptly addressing issues before they escalate prevents misalignment and builds trust within the team. This proactive approach to feedback management ensures that all voices are heard and valued.

Immediately address conflict and don't let it fester

Effective conflict resolution is pivotal in maintaining team cohesion. Instituting processes that focus on common goals and constructive dialogue helps resolve disagreements without assigning blame, ensuring that the team remains united in the face of challenges.

Engage informal leaders

Identifying and empowering informal leaders within the team can amplify the project's message and drive change more effectively.

These change champions can influence their peers and contribute to a culture of alignment and commitment.

Be rigorous in your use of agendas

This sounds basic but it is worth mastering. Structuring meetings with clear agendas and following up with rigorous action summaries ensures that time is spent on priority topics. This disciplined approach to meetings keeps the team focused on the most critical issues and drives progress towards the project's goals.

Recognise contribution openly

Publicly acknowledging and thanking team members who go above and beyond, and who contribute to alignment and project success fosters a positive culture of recognition. This not only motivates individuals but also sets a standard for the behaviours that are valued within the team.

PART FOUR | IMPLEMENT

Chapter 11: Turnaround Planning

This phase marks a critical point in the strategic evolution of an organisation, especially regarding its sales operations. It goes beyond a mere procedural step, translating strategic vision and priorities into concrete objectives, initiatives, and execution plans. This involves a detailed orchestration of the organisation's strategic vision into actionable and measurable goals, requiring a comprehensive execution roadmap that aligns all resources and stakeholders, supported by a strong governance model for oversight.

The importance of thorough planning as the foundation for directing efforts over the next 6-12-24 months, ensuring alignment and accountability within the sales organisation and its partners, is fundamental. Turnaround Planning allows organisations to systematically turn strategic visions into actionable objectives and initiatives. This process involves setting short-term objectives with OKRs, assembling cross-functional teams, developing an integrated 18–24-month roadmap, creating resource plans and budgets, and establishing governance models. This structured approach is supported by quantitative success metrics, coordinated schedules and budgets, and effective oversight.

When properly implemented, Turnaround Planning aligns resources towards achieving improvement programmes, promoting alignment, accountability, and adaptability, thus laying the groundwork for strategic change.

Step 1: Defining Strategic Objectives and Key Results (OKRs)

The first stage involves defining the strategic objectives and key results that will frame the Turnaround effort. This requires drafting 2-3 ambitious and measurable objectives for the 6–12-month timeframe. Each objective should be accompanied by quantitative key results that will determine whether the objective is achieved. Together, the OKRs create a measurable goal framework for the turnaround.

Step 2: Forming Cross-Functional Delivery Teams

With the objectives defined, cross-functional delivery teams need to be formed to execute the key initiatives. These teams should have an appropriate mix of skills, leveraging talent from different areas of the organisation. The teams should be fully empowered to drive progress on initiatives while maintaining alignment with the overarching strategy.

Step 3: Mapping the Turnaround Roadmap

The next step is mapping out an integrated turnaround roadmap over an 18–24-month timeline. This outlines the sequencing of all the strategic initiatives and Turnaround programmes identified. Their interdependencies should be coordinated, and major milestones need to be delineated across the timeline for effective tracking.

Step 4: Constructing Detailed Resource Plans and Budgets

This stage involves constructing detailed resource plans and budgets to support execution. Bottom-up plans need to be developed across all areas including talent, technology, facilities, and other dimensions. Additionally, an integrated profit and loss budget must be created that aligns capital to the strategic priorities.

Step 5: Designing Governance Standards and Forums

The final stage focuses on instituting governance mechanisms for managing and tracking the Turnaround effort. This starts by defining a comprehensive governance structure that clearly specifies decision rights and accountabilities. Additionally, periodic steering committee meetings need to be established for executive oversight. Finally, routines and forums for initiative monitoring, status reviews, and mid-course corrections should be created.

Integral to this governance structure is the implementation of a RACI (Responsible, Accountable, Consulted, Informed) matrix to clarify roles and responsibilities across all stages of the turnaround process. The RACI framework ensures that every task, decision, and initiative has a clearly designated individual or team responsible for its execution, an accountable party ensuring its completion, stakeholders who are consulted during the process, and those who are informed of outcomes and progress. This clarity in roles and responsibilities is crucial for maintaining organisational alignment, facilitating effective communication, and ensuring accountability throughout the Turnaround journey. By embedding the RACI model within the governance standards, organisations can enhance the efficiency and effectiveness of their planning, ensuring that strategic objectives are met with precision and in alignment with the overall vision.

PART FOUR | IMPLEMENT

Chapter 12: Pilot Testing
& Training

The phased rollout beginning with a pilot is a critical step in the Turnaround journey, acting as a bridge between planning and full-scale implementation. This approach validates the effectiveness of the change elements and fosters a culture of agility, learning, and continuous improvement. Here are the best practices for a successful pilot rollout:

1. Start with a small, willing pilot group and co-create the programme with inputs from frontline sales teams to drive greater buy-in and feasibility. Allow for a minimum duration of 8-12 weeks to enable sufficient time for meaningful capability building and refinements.

2. Conduct intensive "train-the-trainer" certifications to ensure coaching and facilitation staff have complete capability uplift and accreditation on programme content and methodologies prior to launch. Equip them with user-friendly digital tools, content asset repositories, messaging templates, and reusable coaching agenda templates aligned to the blueprint to support consistent delivery.

3. Clearly define a structured coaching blueprint detailing specific touchpoints, rhythms, and coaching methods. Ensure sales leadership shadowing for designated shoulder-to-shoulder coaching early during programme launch to provide leadership visibility and reinforcement messaging.

4. Establish specific quantitative success metrics tied to clear revenue, customer acquisition, employee engagement, and sales representative performance goals. Holistically evaluate adoption outcomes across people, process adoption, and technology utilisation dimensions.

5. Assign dedicated change management resourcing to support continuous multi-channel communication with participants, systematically capture feedback on effectiveness, and enable rapid iteration of content or coaching. Schedule clear milestone check-ins at 4 weeks and 8 weeks for assessment.

6. Quantitatively assess capability uplift pre- and post-pilot through assessments, analytics, and participant interviews to identify gaps. Capture structured feedback from pilot participants on the effectiveness of the coaching/facilitation staff support at regular intervals.

7. Establish communities of practice for coaching/facilitation staff across delivery locations to share best practices, insights, tools, and learnings from their pilot delivery experiences.

8. Thoroughly document key learnings, challenges, recommendations, and best practices that emerge throughout the piloting phase to inform refinement of the programme design, content, and full national rollout strategy.

By carefully selecting cross-functional teams to run pilot projects, obtaining and integrating feedback, and making necessary adjustments, organisations can significantly enhance the likelihood of a successful turnaround. This approach sets the stage for the successful realisation of strategic objectives in the next phase of the turnaround.

PART FOUR | IMPLEMENT

Chapter 13: Programme Rollout

The rollout is a pivotal juncture in the sales turnaround programme, transitioning from pilot testing to full-scale implementation across the entire sales organisation. It is crucial for realising the strategic vision of the turnaround and ensuring the benefits observed during the pilot are replicated and sustained throughout the organisation. Meticulous planning, robust change management strategies, and unwavering leadership commitment are essential to navigate the complexities of scaling the turnaround initiatives.

Rollout is always intense and can resemble an emergency room in a hospital at its worst. The logistics management is usually nothing short of brutal, encompassing administration, scheduling, coordination, event management, programme delivery, implementation of technologies and processes, and project management. A structured, disciplined, and rigorous approach to change management is required, including monitoring and tracking of metrics, communication, feedback, training, and support mechanisms to facilitate the adoption of new practices, technologies, and behaviours across the sales teams. Both successes and failures need to be quickly identified and acted upon.

The rollout phase is guaranteed to be complex yet rewarding. It is rewarding because one watches one's work come to life, and it is complex because one is dealing with human beings, who are infinitely complex creatures, and change exacerbates that.

The opportunities inherent in getting it right are many, including:

1. Enhanced and rapidly improving sales performance as teams are injected with energy and the promise of success and commensurate rewards

2. Increased operational efficiency, reducing costs and improving productivity and overall effectiveness of the sales organisation through streamlined sales processes and removal of inefficiencies

3. Improved employee engagement, cohesion, and morale, resulting in an infectious vibe and reduced turnover

Change Management and Communication

Effective change management is the linchpin of a successful organisation-wide rollout. It involves structure, organisation, and coordination, as well as a comprehensive communication strategy that articulates the vision, benefits, and expectations of the turnaround to all stakeholders. Clear, consistent, and transparent communication helps mitigate resistance, build buy-in, and foster a positive attitude towards change. Training and development programmes are essential to equip sales teams with the necessary skills and knowledge to adapt to new processes, technologies, and methodologies. Establishing feedback loops and support channels is crucial for addressing concerns, providing guidance, and facilitating a smooth transition.

Technology Integration and Process Optimisation

This is a potential danger area, full of proverbial barbed wire and landmines. Seamless removal and/or integration of technologies into the tech stack is uncommon – there are usually challenges, ranging from unpleasant to excruciating. However, it is vital for enhancing efficiency, improving data-driven decision-making, and boosting productivity and performance. Close collaboration between sales, IT, and operations teams is necessary to ensure technology solutions align with sales objectives and are user-friendly. Process optimisation efforts should focus on streamlining workflows, eliminating redundancies, and embedding best practices into sales operations.

Comprehensive Preparation and Customisation

The rollout phase commences with an exhaustive preparatory stage, ensuring every facet of the sales organisation is primed for the turnaround. This involves customising the rollout plan to accommodate the unique characteristics, challenges, and strengths of different teams, acknowledging diversity in readiness levels, cultural nuances, and operational variances to facilitate smoother adoption and minimise resistance.

Stakeholder Engagement and Leadership Alignment

Engagement and alignment of all stakeholders, particularly leadership at various levels, is central to the success of the rollout. Securing their buy-in and commitment is crucial for driving change from the top down. Leaders serve as champions of the turnaround, embodying change, motivating their teams, and providing necessary support. Regular engagement sessions, workshops, and forums can be instrumental in aligning stakeholders, addressing concerns, and fostering a unified vision.

Monitoring, Evaluation, and Continuous Improvement

As things roll, continuous monitoring and evaluation are imperative to track progress, measure impact, and identify areas for further improvement. Key performance indicators (KPIs) and metrics defined during the strategic planning phase should be used to assess effectiveness and impact. A data-driven approach enables timely adjustments and refinements to the strategy, ensuring alignment with evolving business objectives and market conditions. Fostering a culture of continuous improvement encourages innovation and agility within the sales organisation.

Best Practices for Organisation-wide Rollout

1. **Incremental Deployment:** Adopting an incremental approach to the rollout can significantly mitigate risks by segmenting the rollout into manageable phases, allowing for real-time adjustments and minimising disruption to ongoing operations.

2. **Comprehensive Training and Support:** Ensuring all members of the sales organisation are well-prepared for the changes through initial training sessions and ongoing support mechanisms, including help desks, FAQs, and peer mentoring systems.

3. **Clear Communication:** Transparent, consistent, and clear communication throughout the rollout process, keeping stakeholders at every level informed about progress, expectations, and adjustments to the plan.

4. **Stakeholder Engagement:** Engaging with stakeholders early and often to identify potential resistance, address concerns proactively, and leverage their insights for a more effective rollout.

5. **Robust Feedback Loops:** Establishing mechanisms to gather feedback from all levels of the sales organisation and the impacted ecosystem, actively using feedback to tweak and improve the rollout process.

6. **Integration into Daily Operations:** Ensuring the turnaround's principles, processes, and tools become part of the daily routines and workflows of the sales team, aligning new practices with overall business objectives.

7. **Continuous Learning and Development:** Establishing ongoing training programmes to build skills, introduce advanced concepts, and ensure the sales team remains proficient and adapts to evolving market demands.

8. **Culture of Continuous Improvement:** Cultivating a culture that encourages experimentation, feedback, and iterative changes, recognising and rewarding innovation and resilience in the face of challenges.

9. **Vocal Leadership Commitment:** Continued support and commitment from leadership, expressed publicly and often, to embed and sustain the turnaround, exemplifying new ways of working and actively promoting the turnaround's values.

10. **Success Stories and Case Studies:** Sharing success stories and case studies from within the organisation to illustrate the practical benefits of the turnaround, motivating others to embrace the changes.

Threats and Dangers

When trying to roll out the programme and juggling a million balls, putting out fires, placating egos, and cleaning up messes, watch out for these key threats:

1. **Resistance to Change:** One of the most significant threats to a successful rollout, stemming from a lack of understanding, fear of the unknown, or perceived threats to job security.

2. **Inadequate Training:** Failure to provide comprehensive training and support can lead to confusion, errors, and a lack of adoption of new systems and processes.

3. **Poor Communication:** Inadequate communication results in misinformation, uncertainty, distrust, and a lack of engagement from the sales team, undermining the success of the rollout.

4. **Overlooking Feedback:** Ignoring feedback from the sales team and their collaborators leads to missed opportunities for improvement at best and outright failure at worst.

5. **Underestimating the Demands:** Underestimating the demands, requirements, and overall complexity of the rollout can lead to insufficient planning and resource allocation, jeopardising the success of the turnaround.

6. **Political fallout:** The reasons for political fallout (when powerful people go to war) can be as numerous as the grains of sand on a beach. It's a big threat compounded by a lack of information.

7. **Complacency:** One of the significant risks during this phase, where initial successes lead to a decrease in momentum and a return to old habits.

8. **Lack of Continued Support:** Insufficient ongoing support and resources for the turnaround can lead to its gradual erosion, undermining the investments made during the rollout phase.

9. **Resistance to Continuous Improvement:** An organisational culture that resists continuous improvement and feedback can stifle innovation and the long-term sustainability of the turnaround.

Momentum

Maintaining momentum throughout the turnaround is critical in the true sense of the word. Cultivate it, accelerate it, and protect it for all you are worth. Momentum is the energy and drive that keeps the turnaround alive, vibrant, and moving towards its ultimate goals. It embodies the collective enthusiasm, commitment, and action of all stakeholders involved, ensuring the turnaround maintains its course, fosters a culture of change and adaptability, and generates a sense of urgency and purpose.

Several factors can accelerate momentum in a turnaround programme:

- **Strong Leadership:** Visionary and committed leadership provides direction and inspires confidence, driving momentum by aligning and mobilising stakeholders towards common goals.

- **Clear Communication:** Transparent and consistent communication about the turnaround's purpose, progress, and successes helps build trust and buy-in, fuelling momentum.

- **Quick Wins:** Identifying and achieving quick wins early in the turnaround process can boost morale and demonstrate the benefits of change, thereby accelerating momentum.

- **Stakeholder Engagement:** Actively involving employees, customers, and other stakeholders in the turnaround process ensures their commitment and participation, driving momentum forward.

- **Adaptability:** Being able to quickly adapt strategies and plans in response to feedback and changing conditions keeps the turnaround relevant and maintains its forward thrust.

Conversely, several factors can impede momentum:

- **Resistance to Change:** Organisational inertia and individual resistance to change can slow down or derail turnaround efforts.

- **Lack of Alignment:** Misalignment between the turnaround goals and the organisation's culture, values, or business objectives can hinder progress.

- **Resource Constraints:** Insufficient resources, whether financial, human, or technological, can stall turnaround initiatives.

- **Poor Communication:** Ambiguity or lack of communication about the turnaround's vision, benefits, and progress can lead to confusion and disengagement.

PART FOUR | IMPLEMENT

Chapter 14: Turnaround Performance and ROI

Without measuring and monitoring progress, the recognition that change leaders deserve will never materialise. Being metrics-focused and performance-monitoring obsessed is crucial for galvanising, controlling, and aligning the many divergent factors and forces that naturally pull in different directions. This section outlines how to approach choosing metrics and reporting on them to ensure project success. Each of the 15 core metrics discussed in this section plays a vital role in assessing current sales performance and informing sales turnaround strategies. This chapter addresses issues related to metric limitations, choices, and setup, and discusses the utility of a North Star Metric. It first establishes a shared understanding of their importance and differences, enabling informed decision-making to drive growth and adapt to changing market dynamics.

The debate over the primacy and fundamental importance of sales metrics in the B2B business context is nuanced and multifaceted. Key metrics consistently utilised include Total Sales Revenue, Sales Growth Rate, and New Sales Revenue, with Annual Recurring Revenue added if subscription models are relevant. For early-stage or growth companies, metrics such as Customer Lifetime Value and Customer Acquisition Cost, along with the ratio between them, are typically standard. These metrics serve distinct yet interconnected roles in evaluating a company's sales performance. While this section does not attempt to settle the debate around their importance or primacy, it delves into the significance of each of the 15 chosen metrics and how they collectively contribute to a comprehensive understanding of a company's health and growth trajectory.

1. Total Annual Sales Revenue offers a comprehensive overview of financial performance and market presence. It reflects the company's ability to generate revenue across all sources and is crucial for broad financial health and operational scale assessment through year-over-year growth analysis.

2. New Sales Revenue measures the effectiveness of market expansion and customer acquisition strategies, focusing solely on new business to evaluate the impact of new sales initiatives.

3. Annual Recurring Revenue (ARR) assesses the stability of revenue streams in subscription models. It provides insight into financial health and business model sustainability, focusing on customer retention and revenue predictability.

4. Sales Growth Rate evaluates the company's growth trajectory. It encompasses all sales revenue sources, highlighting trends and potential strategic adjustments, with comparative analysis identifying growth trends.

5. Customer Lifetime Value (CLV) guides strategic decisions on customer acquisition and retention. It focuses on the revenue potential from each customer, maximising profitability and efficiency in customer relationship management.

6. Customer Acquisition Cost (CAC) evaluates the efficiency of acquisition strategies. Limited to new customer acquisition costs, it reveals the investment required for new customers and assesses trends in acquisition efficiency.

7. Customer Retention Rate assesses customer satisfaction and retention strategies. Focused on existing customer base retention, it indicates the company's success in maintaining relationships and loyalty.

8. Conversion Rate assesses the sales funnel's effectiveness. It applies to the entire sales funnel, optimising sales process and marketing efforts, evaluated periodically to identify conversion efficiency improvements or declines.

9. Average Sales Cycle gauges sales process efficiency. Encompassing the entire sales process, it aims to reduce time to close and increase sales efficiency, tracking changes over time to assess process improvements.

10. Average Order Value (AOV) understands customer buying behaviour. It indicates upselling and cross-selling strategy effectiveness, focusing on increasing revenue per transaction through strategic pricing and sales tactics.

11. Forecast Accuracy is a pivotal metric that gauges the precision of sales forecasts against actual sales, highlighting the sales team's effectiveness in opportunity qualification and sales execution. It serves as a crucial indicator of the sales operation's analytical prowess and its ability to allocate resources efficiently, manage inventory, and plan financially.

12. Net Promoter Score (NPS) measures customer loyalty based on their likelihood to recommend the company. It gauges overall customer sentiment and loyalty, enhancing customer experience across all touchpoints, with regular assessments tracking sentiment changes.

13. Pipeline Value forecasts potential future revenue. It encompasses all pipeline stages, focusing on sales forecasting and resource allocation, with dynamic assessment reflecting real-time pipeline changes.

14. Sales Velocity measures sales process efficiency. Covering the entire sales process, it focuses on accelerating sales and improving conversion rates, tracking efficiency improvements or declines over time.

15. Sales Velocity Index compares current sales velocity against a baseline to assess performance changes. It benchmarks sales process efficiency over time, focusing on continuous sales process and strategy improvement, with direct comparison to baseline periods quantifying efficiency changes.

Where to Start

Embarking on a sales turnaround project as a change leader, especially when faced with insufficient data or unsophisticated tracking systems at the client's end, requires a strategic and adaptable approach. The objective is twofold: obtaining benchmark data for tracking performance improvements and selecting a set of metrics crucial for measuring success and ROI.

To navigate this complex and tricky priority in the overall turnaround:

1: Establish Benchmark Data

Identify Available Data: Start by assessing what data the client currently collects and has access to. Even if they don't track all 15 metrics, there might be some basic sales, customer, or financial data that can serve as a starting point. Push through the client's embarrassment at having poor data available. If things are bad, expect them to be evasive and even avoidant. Push through this and obtain what is available or forfeit vital ROI.

Prioritise Key Metrics: Based on the initial assessment, prioritise metrics that are essential for the sales turnaround project and can be calculated with available data. For instance, Total Annual Sales Revenue, New Sales Revenue, and Customer Retention Rate might be simpler to track and highly relevant for most turnarounds, and you are guaranteed to be able to work out Sales Growth Rate from there.

Implement Data Collection Methods: For missing but crucial metrics, work with the client to implement new data collection methods. This might involve setting up basic tracking in their CRM system, using spreadsheets for manual tracking, or adopting affordable sales analytics tools that don't require sophisticated tech setups.

Use Industry Benchmarks: When internal historical data is scarce, industry benchmarks can provide a valuable reference point. Research industry reports, case studies, or use benchmarking services to gather data on average performance metrics in the client's sector.

2: Choose Metrics That Matter

Align Metrics with Objectives: The selection of metrics should directly align with the specific objectives of the sales turnaround project. If the goal, apart from growth which is always front of mind, is to improve sales efficiency, metrics like Sales Velocity and Conversion Rate might be most relevant. For a focus on profitability, Gross Margin and Average Order Value could be key.

Consider Data Feasibility: Ensure the chosen metrics are feasible for the client to track, given their current technological and operational constraints. It's better to start with a smaller set of critical metrics that can be accurately measured and expanded as their capabilities grow.

Educate and Train: Part of the turnaround process should involve educating the client's team on the importance of these metrics and training them on data collection and analysis methods. This capacity-building approach ensures the sustainability of the turnaround efforts.

Set Up a Reporting Framework: Develop a simple yet effective reporting framework that allows the client to regularly monitor these metrics. The framework should include baseline measurements, targets, and a schedule for regular review and adjustment.

3: Address Data Quality and Maturity Challenges

Data Cleaning Initiatives: If poor data quality is a concern, initiate data cleaning projects to improve the accuracy of existing databases. This might involve standardising data entry processes, cleaning up legacy data, and implementing data validation rules.

Leverage External Expertise: In cases where the client lacks the technical sophistication, consider bringing in external tech support or leveraging cloud-based sales analytics platforms that offer data integration and analytics services without heavy IT infrastructure requirements.

Adopt a Phased Approach: Start with metrics that can be tracked with minimal technological intervention and gradually introduce more sophisticated metrics as the client's capabilities improve. This phased approach helps in building momentum and demonstrating early wins, which is crucial for the success of the turnaround project.

Focus on Cultural Change: Beyond the technical aspects, driving a cultural change towards a data-driven mindset within the client's organisation is crucial. Encourage leadership to champion the importance of data and analytics in decision-making processes.

By carefully navigating these steps, you can effectively tackle the challenges of benchmarking and metric selection in sales turnaround projects, even in environments with limited data sophistication or technological capabilities. The key is to start with what's available, prioritise for impact, and build towards sophistication through education, cultural change, and strategic technology adoption.

Monitoring, Tracking, and Reporting on Progress

Monitoring, tracking, and reporting on the impact and effectiveness of a sales turnaround project, especially during its progression, is crucial for maintaining transparency, ensuring alignment, and driving decision-making. When preparing for a SteerCo meeting, which typically involves senior and busy stakeholders, it's essential to present information that is concise, impactful, and visually engaging. Fail to do this and you are likely to be chewed up and spat out, and that is no joking matter.

1: Preparing the Dashboard

Focus on Key Metrics: Select 5-7 key metrics that directly align with the project's objectives and are most indicative of its success. These could include Sales Growth Rate, Conversion Rate, Customer Acquisition Cost (CAC), Customer Retention Rate, and Sales Velocity. The choice of metrics should reflect the project's focus areas and what the SteerCo values most. Consultation with the project team before the first SteerCo in order to get a green light for choices is advised.

Design for Clarity: Use a clean, easy-to-read layout for your dashboard. Each metric should have its own section or widget. Utilise clear labels, consistent colour schemes, and avoid clutter. Tools like Power BI, Tableau, or even Excel can be used to create visually appealing dashboards.

Incorporate Trend Data: For each metric, include not just the current value but also trend data over the project's duration. Use line graphs for trends, bar charts for comparisons, and gauges for target achievements. This helps in visualising progress and identifying patterns.

Highlight Benchmarks and Targets: Where applicable, include industry benchmarks or pre-project performance levels alongside current data to contextualise improvements. Clearly mark targets for each metric so achievements can be easily assessed at a glance.

Ensure Real-Time or Regularly Updated Data: If possible, link your dashboard to live data sources. If real-time data isn't feasible, ensure the dashboard is updated before each SteerCo meeting to reflect the latest figures.

2: Using the Dashboard in SteerCo Meetings

Start with High-Level Insights: Begin your presentation with a summary of the most critical insights from the dashboard. Highlight significant achievements and areas of concern in broad strokes to capture attention and set the stage. Generate engagement and positive buzz.

Drill Down into Specific Metrics: After the overview, delve into each key metric. Explain the current performance versus targets, and the trend since the last meeting. Use this as an opportunity to tell the story of the project's progress.

Highlight Victories: Use the dashboard to spotlight significant wins, such as hitting or exceeding a target metric. Briefly discuss the strategies or actions that led to these successes to reinforce what's working.

Flag Concerns and Risks: Identify any metrics that are off-target or trending negatively. Use this as a segue into discussing potential risks or issues impacting the project. Be prepared with analysis and recommendations for addressing these challenges.

Discuss Issues and Resolutions: For any previously reported issues, update the SteerCo on the current status. Use the dashboard to show the impact of resolved issues on project metrics, if applicable.

Facilitate Discussion and Decision-Making: Use the dashboard as a tool to guide discussion. Ask for input on strategic decisions, particularly in areas where the project may be facing challenges. The visual nature of the dashboard can help stimulate conversation and focus the discussion on facts and figures.

Action Items and Next Steps: Conclude the presentation by summarising action items, owner responsibilities, and deadlines. If specific metrics require attention, outline the steps planned to address them before the next meeting.

3: Best Practices for SteerCo Presentation

Keep it Interactive: If the technology allows, use an interactive dashboard that lets you drill down into specific data points or filter data during the presentation. This can be particularly useful for answering questions or exploring scenarios live.

Practice Brevity: Given the time constraints, be bright, be brief and then be gone as a friend used to say. Respect the seniority and time of the audience, practice delivering your insights succinctly. Prepare to elaborate only if questions arise.

Solicit Feedback: Encourage feedback on the dashboard's format and the presentation's content to continuously refine your approach based on the SteerCo's preferences and needs.

By following these guidelines, anyone driving a sales turnaround can effectively communicate the progress and impact of sales turnaround projects to senior stakeholders, ensuring that the SteerCo meetings are productive, focused, and conducive to strategic decision-making. You will also avoid the sharp criticism that always follows if you are unprepared or fumble the presentation in any way.

The Utility of a North Star Metric

A North Star Metric is a singular, overarching metric that the turnaround team (and company) can use to guide its growth and measure its success over time. It represents the core value that the sales organisation delivers to its customers, encapsulating the essence of the turnaround's objectives in a measurable form. The value of a North Star Metric lies in its ability to focus the organisation's efforts and resources on what truly matters, ensuring that all departments and teams in the sales engine are aligned towards a common goal. It galvanises people and teams, simplifies decision-making, enhances strategic alignment, and drives cohesive action across the company.

Choosing a North Star Metric for Sales Turnaround Success

Identifying and rallying around a North Star Metric can effectively focus efforts and measure success. This metric should encapsulate the essence of the turnaround's goals, serving as a beacon for all activities and decisions. Here's how to select this pivotal metric:

1. **Align with Turnaround Goals:** Choose a metric that directly reflects the primary objective of the sales turnaround, whether it's enhancing customer engagement, increasing sales efficiency, or improving product-market fit.

2. **Simplify to Amplify:** Select a metric that simplifies complex processes into a single, understandable figure, making it easier for everyone to grasp what matters most and align their efforts accordingly.

3. **Ensure Measurability:** The chosen metric should be easily measurable and trackable over time, allowing for regular updates to keep the team informed and motivated.

4. **Drive Actionable Insights:** Pick a metric that not only measures success but also drives actionable insights, helping identify what's working and what needs adjustment.

5. **Facilitate Team Alignment:** The North Star Metric should be relevant to all team members, providing a common goal that unites their efforts across departments.

6. **Promote Engagement and Motivation:** Choose a metric that can galvanise the team, fostering a sense of ownership and commitment to the turnaround's success.

Implementing the North Star Metric

- **Communicate Clearly and Consistently:** Once selected, communicate the North Star Metric to all stakeholders, explaining its importance and how it will guide the turnaround. Regular communication about progress keeps the team focused and motivated.

- **Integrate into Daily Operations:** Make the North Star Metric a part of daily conversations, meetings, and decision-making processes to ensure it remains at the forefront of everyone's mind and actions.

- **Celebrate Milestones:** Recognise and celebrate significant progress towards the North Star Metric to boost morale and reinforce the value of everyone's contributions.

Sales Velocity: The Ideal North Star Metric?

Sales Velocity is arguably the ideal North Star Metric for a sales turnaround project, assuming the necessary data and analytics are in place. This comprehensive composite metric measures the speed at which a company converts leads into revenue, encapsulating four critical components:

1. **Number of Opportunities:** Total deals within a given period

2. **Average Deal Size:** Average expected revenue per sale

3. **Win Rate:** Percentage of opportunities converted into sales

4. **Length of Sales Cycle:** Average time to close a deal

Sales Velocity aligns every team member and resource with the goal of increasing revenue efficiently and effectively. It represents the essence of successful sales turnarounds: faster, more profitable sales resulting from collaborative efforts across the company.

Mathematically, Sales Velocity is calculated by multiplying the number of opportunities, average deal size, and win rate, then dividing by the length of the sales cycle. This represents the average daily revenue generated by the sales process, providing insights into the efficiency and effectiveness of sales operations.

Sales Velocity stands out for several reasons:

1. **Direct Impact on Revenue:** It directly ties to revenue generation within a specific timeframe, indicating the turnaround's bottom-line impact.

2. **Encourages Cross-functional Collaboration:** Improving Sales Velocity requires efforts from multiple departments, fostering alignment towards a common goal.

3. **Reflects Efficiency and Effectiveness:** It reflects both the efficiency (sales cycle length) and effectiveness (win rate and deal size) of the sales process.

4. **Offers Actionable Insights:** Breaking down Sales Velocity into components allows teams to identify specific areas for improvement.

5. **Facilitates Agile Adjustments:** Its sensitivity to changes in sales operations enables quick adjustments to strategies and tactics.

6. **Inspires Continuous Improvement:** As a dynamic metric, it motivates teams to continuously optimise the sales process and drive revenue faster.

Beyond Sales Velocity

Beyond Sales Velocity, there are several other composite metrics that can be used as North Star Metrics and that offer valuable insights into different aspects of sales performance. Here are five alternative composite metrics:

1. Customer Acquisition Efficiency (CAE)

CAE = Total Revenue Generated from New Customers divided by the Total Cost of Sales and Marketing for New Customers

Customer Acquisition Efficiency measures how effectively a company is acquiring new customers relative to the costs incurred in sales and marketing efforts. A higher CAE indicates more efficient customer acquisition processes, suggesting that the sales turnaround is leading to more cost-effective growth strategies.

2. Sales Productivity Index (SPI)

SPI = Total Sales Revenue divided by the Number of Sales Representatives

The Sales Productivity Index evaluates the average revenue generated per sales representative. This metric helps in assessing the impact of sales training, tools, and processes introduced during the turnaround. Improvements in SPI signal that sales representatives are becoming more effective and efficient, contributing to overall sales growth.

3. Customer Lifetime Value to Customer Acquisition Cost Ratio (CLV:CAC)

CLV:CAC = Customer Lifetime Value (CLV) divided by the Customer Acquisition Cost (CAC)

This ratio compares the lifetime value of a customer to the cost of acquiring that customer. A higher ratio indicates that the value derived from a customer significantly exceeds the cost to acquire them, highlighting the long-term profitability and sustainability of sales strategies implemented during the turnaround.

4. Sales Efficiency Ratio (SER)

SER = New Revenue Generated divided by Sales and Marketing Expenses

Sales Efficiency Ratio measures the return on investment for sales and marketing expenses. It shows how effectively these expenses are converted into new revenue. An increasing SER suggests that the sales turnaround initiatives are enhancing the ROI of sales and marketing efforts, making the operation more efficient.

5. Opportunity Win Rate (OWR)

OWR = Number of Opportunities Won divided by the Total Number of Opportunities

Opportunity Win Rate calculates the percentage of sales opportunities that result in a win (sale). This metric provides insights into the effectiveness of the sales funnel and qualification process. An improvement in OWR post-turnaround indicates that sales strategies and processes are more aligned with customer needs and market demands, leading to a higher success rate in closing deals.

Summary Points

Addressing Return on Investment (ROI) is crucial when discussing sales turnaround projects with the Steering Committee (SteerCo) and Project Sponsors. ROI encapsulates the financial return and serves as an indicator of the project's success and efficiency. Here's how to approach, calculate, validate, distribute, and publicise ROI:

1. **Set Clear Expectations:** Define what constitutes a successful ROI based on industry standards, past performance, or projected outcomes. Engage in open discussions to align expectations regarding ROI targets and timelines.

2. **Establish ROI Calculation Methodology:** Use a simple, consistent formula: (Net Gain from Investment − Cost of Investment)/Cost of Investment x 100. Document the methodology and ensure stakeholder agreement.

3. **Leverage Core Metrics:** Utilise improvements in the 15-core metrics to quantify gains. Identify and track relevant metrics throughout the turnaround to feed into ROI calculation.

4. **Ensure Data Integrity:** Implement strict data validation processes and regularly audit data to maintain accuracy and reliability, building trust in ROI figures.

5. **Address Attribution and Causation:** Document initiatives and their expected impact on key metrics. Use quantitative data

and qualitative feedback to build a case for attribution, while being transparent about limitations.

6. **Seek Leadership Endorsement:** Involve the leadership team in the attribution process, presenting evidence and seeking their endorsement to gain organisation-wide acceptance.

7. **Conduct Scenario Analysis:** Perform scenario analyses to validate ROI under different conditions, considering best-case, worst-case, and most likely scenarios to demonstrate a thorough approach.

8. **Communicate Strategically:** Develop a plan to share ROI achievements with broader audiences using engaging visuals. Highlight key drivers and actions taken to showcase the value of data-driven decision-making.

9. **Leverage for Future Initiatives:** Document ROI and use it as a benchmark for future projects. Share lessons learned and best practices, and continuously monitor ROI post-turnaround.

10. **Celebrate Success:** Recognise the efforts and contributions of everyone involved when the project achieves or exceeds targeted ROI, boosting morale and reinforcing the importance of the turnaround initiative.

By strategically navigating the ROI landscape and effectively communicating success, change leaders can solidify their reputation, gain organisational support, and drive continuous improvement through data-driven decision-making.

CONCLUSION

As we reach the conclusion of this journey through the intricacies of sales turnaround, it is crucial to reflect on the core principles and insights that weave throughout these pages. The path we've traced - from establishing solid foundations in Chapter 3 through to measuring ROI in Chapter 14 - reveals an inescapable truth: sustainable sales transformation demands a systemic understanding that places the customer journey at its heart.

The diagnostic framework detailed in Chapters 4 and 5 highlighted how seemingly isolated issues often stem from deeper systemic roots. When we examined sales culture in Chapter 6, we saw how cultural patterns ripple through every aspect of the revenue engine. The collaborative alliances explored in Chapter 6 demonstrated the intricate web of relationships that must be nurtured for success. Each chapter has built upon this fundamental recognition of interconnectedness.

Yet perhaps nothing illustrates this systemic nature more vividly than our examination of the customer journey. As explored in Chapter 2, the way customers experience their interactions with an organisation cannot be reduced to individual touchpoints or departmental responsibilities. Their journey cuts across functional boundaries, transcending the artificial silos we create in our organisational charts. A customer doesn't care that their frustration with implementation stems from a disconnect between sales promises and delivery capabilities - they simply experience a broken promise that erodes trust.

This systemic reality demands that transformation efforts be calibrated first and foremost to the customer's experience. The tools and frameworks presented throughout this book - from the governance structures in Chapter 10 to the pilot testing protocols in Chapter 12 - must be wielded with this primary focus. Without it, we risk the all-too-common scenario of achieving impressive operational metrics while leaving fundamental customer pain points unaddressed.

Consider how often organisations invest heavily in sales transformation only to discover that customer satisfaction remains stagnant or even declines. The root cause typically traces back to a fragmented approach that fails to recognize how changes in one area ripple through the entire system. A new CRM implementation might streamline internal processes but add friction to the customer's interaction. Revised compensation structures might drive short-term revenue but incentivise behaviours that damage long-term relationships.

The performance management systems detailed in Chapter 10 and the ROI metrics explored in Chapter 14 must therefore extend beyond traditional sales metrics to encompass the full spectrum of customer experience. This is not merely about measuring customer satisfaction - it's about understanding how each element of the sales engine contributes to or detracts from the customer's journey.

The pilot testing and training approaches outlined in Chapter 12 become particularly crucial in this light. They provide the mechanism for validating that changes truly enhance customer experience rather than simply optimising internal metrics. The programme rollout strategies in Chapter 13 must similarly maintain this customer-centric focus as initiatives scale across the organisation.

But perhaps most importantly, the systems thinking principles introduced in Chapter 1 provide the intellectual framework needed to maintain this holistic perspective. They remind us that no element of the sales engine exists in isolation. Every process change, every technology implementation, every cultural shift sends ripples through the entire system - ripples that ultimately manifest in the customer's experience.

This brings us to a crucial point about transformation leadership. The consulting and client teams discussed in Chapter 9 must serve as guardians of this systemic perspective. Their role is not simply to implement changes but to anticipate and manage the complex web of interdependencies that determine success. They must constantly ask: How will this change impact the customer's journey? What unintended consequences might emerge? Where might problems resurface in new forms?

The pricing execution challenges explored in Chapter 13 offer a perfect example. Pricing decisions impact not just immediate revenue but customer perceptions, sales team behavior, competitive positioning, and long-term relationship potential. A systemically-aware approach considers all these dimensions rather than optimising for any single metric.

Looking ahead, the proliferation of digital tools and AI-powered capabilities discussed in the Foreword only increases the importance of this systemic perspective. As our technological capabilities grow, so too does the potential for both positive and negative ripple effects through the system. The key is harnessing these tools in service of an integrated customer experience rather than letting them drive further fragmentation.

For sales leaders embarking on transformation journeys, this book offers both a warning and a promise. The warning is clear: piecemeal approaches that ignore systemic realities will fail to deliver sustainable improvement. The promise is equally clear: by embracing a holistic approach grounded in customer experience, genuine transformation becomes possible.

The frameworks, methodologies, and insights shared in these pages provide the tools needed for this journey. From the deep analysis protocols of Chapter 4 to the capability building approaches of Chapter 8, each element has been designed to support systemic transformation. But tools alone are not enough - they must be wielded with consistent awareness of their systemic impact.

This is ultimately a call for a fundamental shift in how we approach sales transformation. Rather than starting with internal metrics or operational efficiency, we must begin with the customer's journey. Rather than optimising individual components, we must focus on the health of the entire system. Rather than accepting quick fixes, we must invest in sustainable solutions that address root causes.

The transformation journey itself must mirror these principles. As detailed in Chapters 10 through 13, successful implementation requires careful attention to governance, testing, training, and rollout. Each phase must maintain focus on the ultimate goal: creating a sales engine that consistently delivers value through every customer interaction.

For those ready to embark on this journey, the path forward is clear if challenging. It begins with truly understanding your customer's journey - not just the touchpoints you've designed but the actual experience they encounter. It requires honest assessment of how your current systems help or hinder that journey. It demands willingness to challenge assumptions and reshape operations around customer needs.

The reward for this effort is transformation that sticks - change that delivers sustainable improvement rather than temporary gains. By aligning your entire sales engine around customer experience, you create the foundation for lasting success. The metrics detailed in Chapter 14 will improve not because you've targeted them directly, but because you've built a system that naturally generates better outcomes.

This is the ultimate lesson of sales transformation: sustainable improvement comes not from optimising individual metrics but from creating a coherent system that consistently delivers value to customers. Every element explored in this book - from strategy to structure, from process to technology, from culture to capability - must serve this higher purpose.

The journey ahead will not be easy. True transformation never is. But armed with the systemic understanding and practical tools provided in these pages, you have what you need to begin. The question is not whether transformation is possible, but whether you are ready to embrace the holistic approach it demands.

Your customers are waiting. Their journey through your organisation continues whether you optimise it or not. The choice now is whether to take control of that journey, to shape it intentionally through systemic transformation, or to let it evolve haphazardly with all the missed opportunities that implies.

The frameworks are here. The methodologies are proven. The path is clear. The time for transformation is now.

ABOUT THE AUTHOR

Mark C. Ward is the CEO and Founder of Revenue Arc, a management consulting firm dedicated to unlocking sales performance and accelerating revenue growth for investor-backed technology companies and B2B businesses. With over two decades of experience driving growth and transforming sales organisations for some of the world's most recognised brands, Mark has established himself as a sales turnaround specialist and a thought leader in the field of enterprise sales.

Mark's expertise spans multiple industries, but he is most at home on the frontiers of technology. His client roster ranges from ambitious investor-backed start-ups to Fortune 500 giants, demonstrating his ability to navigate and optimise sales systems of varying complexities. As the creator of Impact-Centric Selling, a methodology designed specifically for enterprise sales, Mark has developed a powerful framework for improving sales performance and driving results.

Throughout his career, Mark has been entrusted with guiding corporate strategy, facilitating M&A integration, and aligning executive teams. His skill as a facilitator has led him to design and lead hundreds of sales kick-offs, a testament to his ability to energise and focus sales teams. Mark's approach is rooted in the belief that sustainable revenue growth is about much more than just sales performance—it's about aligning and optimising the entire revenue system, including go-to-market strategy, structures, processes, roles, technology, and people.

Educationally, Mark holds a BA in Psychology and Communication Science from the University of South Africa, where he graduated with a distinction, and a Master's degree in Property Science from the University of the Free State where he attained the highest honours in the programme. This unique combination of psychology, communication, and business acumen informs his holistic approach to sales transformation.

As the leader of Revenue Arc, Mark has positioned his company to fill a significant gap in the market. Revenue Arc specialises in solving problems at the system level, ensuring that performance improvements and results can endure. Their diagnostic capabilities are designed to unravel even the most complex sales environments, reflecting what Mark calls "systems acuity"—the sharpness and depth of understanding needed to navigate intricate sales systems.

Mark's personal life, professional journey, and innovative approach to sales transformation combine to make him a unique voice in the field of revenue enhancement. His work continues to challenge conventional wisdom and drive meaningful change in how companies approach sales and revenue growth.

www.ingramcontent.com/pod-product-compliance
Lightning Source LLC
Chambersburg PA
CBHW050232270326
41914CB00033BB/1885/J